"*A Journey with Mac* is a delight. Al Katz provides the reader with all the tools necessary to effectively lead an organization. His creative story telling leaves a lasting impression, and helps each of us to absorb his business leadership process. The concepts are not new, yet the approach to solving the most basic and sophisticated business issues is fresh, on target and proven. You will enjoy the ride."

D. Maybank Hagood
President/CEO Southern
Diversified Distributors, Inc.

"Al Katz has taken his extraordinary talent for plain-speak to a new level! *A Journey with Mac* cuts through the complexities and challenges of modern business by returning to the simple core logic from which we all too often stray. Al reveals the tools for success in business – and life – through a fun, readable and well-written tale that will engage and entertain you from the first page."

Pierre Manigault
Chairman of the Board
Evening Post Publishing Company

"*A Journey with Mac* is an inspiring book that's a seamless mixture of Solomon meeting Charles Dickens at the Wharton School of Business...a must-read for business professionals of all ages in all stages of their lives and careers."

Bill Crowe
President & COO, Aretec, Inc.

"In today's world where many get wrapped up in the 'concept-of-the-day' we lose sight of what common sense would require. *A Journey with Mac* presents business basics in an interesting story that not only allows us to grasp and be reminded of these basic concepts but also affords a means to actually employ them."

James I. Kerr, Sr.
Presiden
& Cons

T0117567

"Al Katz writes an extremely practical and entertaining allegory replete with applicable business metaphors that instruct and inspire both entrepreneurs and corporate executives. His message is one of solving the everyday problems of business, some of which are apparent, but many of which are cloaked in the fervor of activity. His thesis is how to put the fun into business and one's personal life; how to rekindle the passion for business, albeit the inherent problems; and how to discover that business and life should be a joy, not drudgery. Al's genius is evident when the reader finds himself in one or more of his characters and predicaments. Full of content, examples and humor, this is a must read for all challenged executives."

Gerry Ogier
President ContraVest

"I am thankful of the day that Al sat on the other side of my desk and asked if I would take a journey with him. *A Journey with Mac* is an insightful, practical gift to help you improve your planning and communication skills. Al's well-crafted story is both engaging and instructive. A must read for those interested in taking their personal and business lives to the next level."

Robert C. Hagood
President, TranSouth Logistics, LLC

"*A Journey with Mac* is an easy and fun read regarding business and management applications that can help any manager of people improve communication, accountability and time management. You will find yourself rooting for the main character Gregg, and may find some similarities in your own life. Al Katz will show you a way to improve your life and help you find a way to have fun again."

Jack R. Krapf, CIMA
The Krapf Group
Merrill Lynch

"WOW. What a brilliantly simple & simply brilliant book about how to have a better business and a better life; with a comfortable & wise friend as a guide."

Ed Pendarvis '65
Founder, Chair Emeritus, Sunbelt Network
Author, "Buying a Business to Secure
Your Financial Freedom"

"Al Katz addresses the common issues that business owners face today in *A Journey with Mac*. He uniquely illustrates the business life cycle that makes every owner ask for more. It is entertaining, wise and a must read."

Karl H. Zerbst, Jr.
Market Leader, Ameris Bank

"From entrepreneurial trailblazer, to academician, to motivational expert, to the ultimate mentor for young minds, Al didn't stop and rest after a first successful career. *A Journey With Mac* may be his highest watermark of all, because it compiles the essence of life lessons he learned along the fascinating way. And Al communicates them thru Mac with humor and simplicity. Thanks for sharing and spreading the joy through this ultimate gift. You will bless millions with this uplift to the next level of life."

Tandy Rice
President Top Billing, Inc.

"*A Journey with Mac* is a great way to learn and/or relearn business fundamentals. The 'real life' cases bring the fundamentals to memorable realism. So many business books make only one salient point, but this book provides many mental hooks for the wealth of fundamentals covered."

Raymond G. Johnson, Jr.
Retired VP of Fibers Manufacturing, Dupont

A Journey With Mac

A Journey With Mac

Rediscovering the Fundamentals of Business

Al Katz

Advantage®

Published by Advantage, Charleston, South Carolina.
Member of Advantage Media Group.

ADVANTAGE is a registered trademark and the Advantage colophon is a trademark of Advantage Media Group, Inc.

Printed in the United States of America.

ISBN: 978-1-59932-079-3
LCCN: 2008926306

Most Advantage Media Group titles are available at special quantity discounts for bulk purchases for sales promotions, premiums, fundraising, and educational use. Special versions or book excerpts can also be created to fit specific needs.

For more information, please write: Special Markets, Advantage Media Group, P.O. Box 272, Charleston, SC 29402 or call 1.866.775.1696.

Table of Contents

Prologue

The camera zoomed in for a close up of the golfer in his familiar red shirt. The HDTV screen brought the reality of the golf game into Gregg's family room while the surround sound captured the murmur of the excited crowd.

Tiger Woods was kneeling behind the ball visualizing its path to the center of the hole. The drama had been mounting for two hours as Woods had pulled within one stroke of the leader. His eight-foot putt had to go into the cup for a birdie to tie the score and give Tiger an opportunity to move into a sudden-death play-off.

Gregg was on the edge of his chair taking in every sight and sound. He watched Tiger stand over the ball focusing on the hole. The crowd was so silent that Gregg thought for a moment that there must be a problem with his speakers. He sat fixated as Tiger stroked the ball and heard someone in the crowd shout, "In the hole!" followed by several echoes repeating the same chant. Tiger was pumping his fist even before the ball dropped into the cup. There would be a play-off!

Gregg settled back ready to watch Tiger and his opponent hit their drives on the first play-off hole. Unexpectedly, Gregg was jolted back into the reality of the day.

"Dad-deee, what are you doing? Come on, get up it's time to go! We're gonna miss the movie," Lucy whined as she tugged Gregg's hand.

Elaine, his wife, tapped her watch pleading, "Come on Gregg or we'll be late!" She paced the floor irritated at Gregg

Gregg felt bombarded. He was being assaulted by the reality of his family simply wanting to go out to eat and enjoy a movie.

Gregg Herbert had been spending this Sunday afternoon trying to relax and watch the Open. Several days' worth of newspapers ringed his chair and stacks of files from work covered the coffee table. He was desperately trying to escape from his chaotic life by imagining himself mingling with the crowd on the golf course. This was only one of Gregg's many diversions he now used to vanish from the world surrounding him.

To say Gregg was conflicted would be an understatement. He felt as if he was being pulled in every direction; like being drawn and quartered. He had not prepared for tomorrow's business meetings. Instead he hid in the excitement of the golf match. He wanted to watch the play-off, but he had promised his family to take them to dinner and a movie. Yes, he felt conflicted. He had broken his last two promises to spend time with Elaine and the girls. In fact, he had missed many of his family's activities.

His two daughters and wife were urging him out of his stupor but Gregg had trouble shifting his thoughts. He felt depressed and drained. He was experiencing major problems in his business, his family was demanding more of his time and his life in general was a bummer. Now in his forties he kept thinking that this was not the way things ought to be. He had lost his direction and focus.

Elaine waited impatiently in her new SUV, fingers drumming on the steering wheel. Completely out of character she took over the driving duties to the restaurant. Tension pricked at Gregg during the drive and it worsened when inside The Bistro they were greeted with a line and a thirty-minute wait. A curt hostess had handed Gregg a pager that would vibrate when their table was ready. Another irritant, another inconvenience!

Gregg's instincts forced him into a conversation with his family as they waited for a table but he had difficulty listening to what was being said. Finally, they were seated and he began to study his menu. After a prolonged silence, Elaine reached over and tipped the top of the menu down so she could see Gregg's face. Noticing how drained he looked she asked in a tone much harsher than she intended, "Gregg, what's wrong? Are you alright?"

"Naw, I'm beat, Hon," Gregg answered wearily.

"But Dad, you just sat around and watched that dumb golf game all afternoon," his sixteen year old daughter added with a smirk. "How tiring could that be?"

"And Daddy, you promised to take us to dinner and a movie and you aren't paying any attention to us," Lucy, eleven, added as she pushed a wisp of hair from her eye.

For the last few months Gregg had placed himself in complete denial. He didn't want to accept how bad his life had become; how draining his business was; how hard he had tried to spend time with his family. Devastated with his plight he finally confessed, "You're right. I don't know what is wrong with me." His admission sounded hollow to him and it didn't make him feel any better.

It was true. Gregg's energy was depleted and his head was filled with too many depressing thoughts. He wanted to get up out of his chair and run as far and as fast as he could. He felt as if he was falling apart in front of his family. *NO!* He screamed mentally. He was supposed to be in charge, the breadwinner, and his family's protector. Tortured by his thoughts, his words came out mechanically and un- convincingly, "Okay, let's eat and head over to the movie." *What's going on with me? Am I going out of my mind?* His thoughts only added to his depression. Numbness settled over him.

Gregg went through the motions of being with his family and Elaine overlooked his mood until they were both getting ready for bed. Glancing at Gregg's reflection in the mirror she asked again, "What's wrong? You've been like this for the last few months and it's getting worse. I love you but I can't stand to see you this way," Elaine said turning around to face him.

"Hon, I wish I knew," he said. Sitting on the bed with his head cradled in his hands he continued, "It seems like my world is caving in. I don't know if I am going through a mid-life crisis, overwhelmed with the business or maybe I'm simply falling apart. I feel so unsettled and I know I'm not connecting with you and the girls."

Elaine panicked hearing Gregg's words. She couldn't handle all the affairs of the family or the responsibilities of their home. She was so dependent on Gregg. What if Gregg couldn't function? What would happen to the business? Terrified, she thought, *what would happen to us?*

Gregg saw Elaine blanch. Walking over to his wife and putting his hands on her shoulders Gregg added, "It's not supposed to be this way. We should be enjoying life. I've worked hard and have almost everything I've ever dreamed of possessing but what I really want is peace of mind—my sanity."

Elaine was frightened because she knew that everything Gregg said was true. If only she could change Gregg back to how he was six months ago.

She hugged Gregg tightly but his weak response gave her no comfort. Pressing her head into his chest she thought, *Could their marriage be coming to an end? Would they lose everything they had worked so hard for? What would happen to her and the girls?* Her knees were shaking and tears filled her eyes. "Gregg what can I do…what can we do?" Elaine asked pleadingly.

Overwhelmed by the events of the evening Elaine watched Gregg get into bed and pull up the covers. Then she headed downstairs and folded herself onto the sofa in the family room. Staring through the French doors into the blackness of her backyard she looked for a sign of encouragement.

Gregg felt his body completely shutting down. The last he remembered thinking before sleep settled over him was, *my life has got to change. I can't deal with this anymore.*

Chapter 1

The alarm shrilled, jolting Gregg from a restless sleep. Groaning, he reached over and hit the snooze button. It was six o'clock on Monday morning—another Monday when he did not want to wake up, get out of bed, or face any part of his day. It was not just that he dreaded this Monday, either. He loathed every working day.

For twenty-three years, Gregg Herbert had worked relentlessly to build his business. Now, after pouring his heart and soul into Herbert and Associates, he felt like he didn't have much to show for all of his years of personal investment. Even though the company had grown considerably since its inception, and even though Gregg lived in an exclusive neighborhood, drove a new Mercedes, and belonged to the local country club, he still didn't feel very fortunate. Even as his own boss with his own company, he had begun to dread going to work; and that anxiety affected every other part of his life.

The alarm clock sounded again, interrupting his discouraging thoughts. Careful not to wake Elaine, he wearily slipped out of bed and walked to the bathroom to begin his morning ritual. During the last several months, he had noticed that his eyes seemed tired-looking. Wrinkle lines had begun to deepen in his brow, and his face sagged. He had missed the last month of working out with his trainer and canceled recent tennis and golf dates; his energy level was at an all-time low.

He turned on the water to give the shower time to steam up, and then went to the sink to shave. As he lathered his face, he began sorting through a mental checklist of the day's calendar. The first item on the agenda was a staff meeting at nine o'clock. Although he dutifully held these meetings, they seemed to him like a waste of time. Nothing much was ever accomplished, and Gregg was not looking forward to either the endless, pointless disagreements that frequently took place or the alternative: a complete lack of response and participation from his staff. What baffled Gregg was that he had handpicked these people and he believed that they were more than capable of doing good work. However, there were serious communication problems between the members of his management team. Most of them had been with the company for many years. They all knew each other well by now, and some had become good friends outside of work; yet despite the familiarity, they were often at each other's throats, blaming each other for the most trivial infractions.

Next on his Monday morning calendar was an orientation meeting at ten o'clock for seven new employees. Employee turnover had been very high in the past few years, and Gregg knew it was expensive and unproductive. What worried him more was the fact that he knew his turnover was a great deal higher than that of other companies in his industry. When he'd asked Kristin, his human resources director, she had listed numerous possible causes that could account for this personnel problem. It was hard to find good people, and apparently the compensation package Herbert and Associates offered was lower than his competitors. But according to exit interviews, there seemed to be no real pattern regarding the employees' decisions to leave.

At noon, he planned to meet Don Paulus, his banker and long-time friend. They were scheduled to have lunch, which should have been something Gregg could look forward to; but he was dreading that meeting, too. He already knew that Don would interrogate him about the company financials, asking him why profits were down when sales were trending upward. Don would inquire as to why he needed to borrow again for operating capital, grill him about what had happened to the company's cash flow, and ask when he planned to start paying off some old debt. Gregg also knew the questions wouldn't end with business. Don was a good friend, close enough to make comments about Gregg's obviously unhealthy lifestyle.

His attention returned to his morning routine. While he had been lost in his depressing thoughts, the mirror had fogged from the shower's steam. A sarcastic thought crossed his mind—maybe it was better if he couldn't see his reflection. He felt completely drained. He knew he was not managing his business well. In fact, he felt like the business had turned on him. He wasn't controlling it; it was controlling him. Straining to see his image through the steam, he questioned if his marriage was falling apart and if there might be a divorce looming to wreck his family.

He reached up to wipe the fog off the mirror, but after a few circular swipes his hand froze in place. It showed the image of another man standing behind him.

Gregg felt a surge of adrenaline pulse through his body as he spun around to face the intruder, who was casually leaning against the wall, arms crossed, as if there were nothing strange about his presence in Gregg's bathroom. He looked to be in his sixties, with a kind face and gentle eyes—he didn't appear menacing at all—but he was still a stranger, trespassing in Gregg's house.

Gregg was about to order the man from his house when he noticed that he carried a well-worn toolbox slung over his shoulder. He was also dressed in bib overalls neatly worn over a clean, starched white shirt, and wisps of gray hair escaped from the denim cap on his head. The thing that baffled Gregg the most was the knowing smile that curled slightly under the man's gray mustache.

Totally perplexed, Gregg voiced the only comment he could muster.

"I don't need anything fixed!"

Hearing the sound of his own voice helped clear his head, and he addressed the intruder again, trying to sound more forceful.

"How did you get into my house? Did my wife hire you? She didn't let me know that you were scheduled to be here today. It's a little early, don't you think?"

"Good morning, Gregg. May I call you Gregg?" The man's voice had a fatherly tone.

Again caught off-guard, Gregg just nodded in agreement. The man looked like a workman, but he certainly didn't sound or carry himself like one.

The stranger smiled. "My name is Mac, and although I'm dressed like a carpenter, my vocation in life is not to fix objects. My purpose is to help fix lives."

Mac paused as if waiting for Gregg to respond, but Gregg, still mystified by the stranger's calm demeanor, remained silent.

Mac continued with his introduction. "Our meeting is not as mysterious as you may think, Gregg. In reality, you have wished for months for such an encounter, although you were not entirely conscious of it."

Gregg shook his head in disbelief. He felt some lingering surges of anger from the fright the man had given him. "I'm damn sure I never wished to meet you in my bathroom at the crack of dawn—with only a towel wrapped around me!"

Mac chuckled softly. "Gregg, haven't you been worried about your business? I know you want to see it improve and not fail. You're spending too much time at the office and not accomplishing much. It's impacting you and your family."

"Well, yes," Gregg answered impatiently. It doesn't take some phony mind reader to determine that. And by the way, if you knew I'd been wishing for these things, why didn't you show up before now? No offense, buddy, but what could you possibly know about my business, or my life, for that matter?" Gregg leaned one hand on the bathroom counter and brought the other one up to his forehead. "I can't believe we're even having this conversation. I must still be asleep…or maybe I'm hallucinating…maybe it really is the beginning of a nervous breakdown for me…."

Mac held up a hand. "Gregg, slow down. Slow down and calm down. First, although this may not seem real to you at this moment, you are not hallucinating. Second, the reason I didn't appear sooner is that you were not ready for me and this visit."

Again Gregg felt his anger escalate, but this time because it seemed all the frustrations of the past weeks and maybe even months, were coming to a head. "Oh, really?" he demanded. "I have been working my butt off all along to make this business grow. If you know so much about me, you should know that this company is extremely important to me. It is my entire life!"

21

His voice continued to rise defensively. "I'm in the office first thing in the morning and I am always the last to leave. I often work on the weekends—which my family complains about—but without all my efforts, there wouldn't be a business. Which means there wouldn't be any way to support my family. It seems I can either provide for them or spend time with them; I can't do both!"

Realizing he might wake Elaine, Gregg lowered his voice and took a deep breath.

Mac had patiently listened until Gregg had finished. Now he said, "Gregg, you are working tirelessly and by all means you are ambitious. You're a good provider for your family. Laziness is not the issue. But, you're at a crossroad. I know you are worried about your business and you want to spend more time with your family. In fact, you've lost the fun and excitement you once enjoyed at work. Don't you want to see things turnaround?"

In his heart, he knew Mac was on target. Mystified at his own reactions, he embraced what he had been fighting in the face of such an unusual situation: an instant connection, as if he could talk to Mac about his problems after they'd only shared a few minutes of conversation. Clearly he needed help, and this man was offering it.

"So, what now, Mac?" he asked bewildered. "What do you want with me?"

Mac's eyes seemed to twinkle. "I told you. My purpose is to help fix lives. I want to show you how you can start to do the same, beginning with your own. What I want right now is for you to take a trip with me."

Gregg started to protest, but Mac held up his hand.

"It won't take long, I promise. You'll be back in no time at all. And when we return, you will know how you can improve your own life and better influence the lives and wellbeing of all those in your company. Think about it. As president of Herbert and Associates, you design the culture of your business and set the tone and example for everyone who enters your doors. Gregg, wouldn't it be great if you could redirect your efforts, spend less time at work, and still have a positive influence on your employees and customers? Now, wouldn't that create some positive changes for you and your business?"

Gregg couldn't help but wonder if this intruder had him under some kind of spell. Regardless, he had almost started to believe the man might be real and that he should listen to his advice. After all, his only alternative was dismal: to ignore this Mac person and just head on to another draining day at the office where nothing changed and what he was doing certainly wasn't working. Besides, if he missed work maybe his absence would at least cause so much chaos among his employees that they would understand how desperately they needed him.

He experienced a moment of indecision, torn between the real and unreal. *I need to get dressed and get to my office. I don't have time for this fantasy*, he thought. Yet somewhere inside he sensed an opportunity presenting itself. He took a moment to splash some water on his face and looked at himself in the mirror for a long moment. He didn't see anything in the eyes that looked back at him that reflected insanity, just the same old weariness and frustration…and maybe, deep down, a glimmer of hope that hadn't been there before.

Finally, still without having resolved what was real and what wasn't, he made his decision.

"Okay, Mac. Let me throw on some clothes." Gregg wondered if he should leave a note for Elaine."

The two men quietly walked downstairs and out the front door, though Gregg paused for a moment in admiration as he saw Mac's vehicle in the driveway: a bright red 1946 Ford pickup that gleamed in the early morning sun.

As he climbed into the passenger's side of the vintage truck, Gregg had no way of knowing it, but he was in for the adventure of a lifetime.

Chapter 2

As Mac navigated through the neighborhood, Gregg felt as though he might well be flying on a magic carpet seated next to a genie. He was still considering the possibility that he was having a very bizarre dream. As they left, Mac seemed relaxed behind the wheel; but while the speedometer displayed a mere thirty-five miles per hour, Gregg had the sensation that the landscape was passing in a blur.

It wasn't long before Mac applied the brakes, and as their surroundings became discernable through the windows, Gregg realized they were already on the edge of town. Before he had time to ask Mac for an explanation, the truck turned into the parking area of Harrison Brothers Electrical Contractors.

It was early enough in the morning that the company had not yet opened for business. However, there were two other cars parked in the lot and the lights were on in the front office; when Mac knocked on the door it was opened immediately.

"Mac! I had a feeling you might be coming today." A thin man with dark hair and intense blue eyes extended his hand. "Come on in. You know we always enjoy your visits. Who have you brought with you this time?"

Mac turned to introduce his companion. "This is Gregg Herbert. Gregg, I'd like you to meet Evan Harrison."

As the two new acquaintances shook hands, another man entered the foyer.

Mac continued the introductions. "This is Evan's younger brother, Graham." Stockier, with a more athletic build, Graham gave Gregg's hand a firm shake.

Gregg scrutinized the brothers. They were about ten years younger than he, and in the presence of their obvious energy he briefly remembered the familiar rush of enjoying what he did. Evan invited everyone into his office, and offered Mac and Gregg coffee.

Mac began to explain things.

"These two brothers are the second generation to own and manage this family business. After their father passed away, they both returned to help their mom with the business. Evan had just finished his MBA, and Graham forfeited his position with State Bank to help him. As you might imagine, neither had any prior experience in the business, and under the circumstances, there wasn't time to train for anything. When I came into this situation, let's just say that Evan and Graham's reaction to my initial visit was about the same as yours, Gregg."

Evan took up where Mac left off. "My brother and I really wanted to be successful with the business and continue our family's legacy. But we were on each other's case almost instantly. We had no focus and no plan, and my dad had kept everything pertaining to the business in his head, so we also didn't have much in the way of company records. Dad knew what was supposed to get done; he basically managed almost everything on his own. We had no clue what we were doing, and we both had different thoughts about how to do it."

Graham agreed. "We were having a beer after work one day when Mac pulled up a barstool next to us and ordered us a round. He seemed like a likeable guy, and we were shocked at how much he knew about us, our family, and our business. Then he took us on a trip similar to the one you have just begun. Gregg, when you return from this journey, nothing will ever be the same. We can promise you that!"

Gregg choked on a bite of the blueberry muffin he was inhaling. Taking a sip of coffee to clear his throat, he said, "You mean, this is all actually real? I mean, it's really happening?"

Evan grinned at his brother. "Sounds a lot like what I said."

Graham smiled at Gregg. "Yes, Gregg, this is really happening. Mac's methods may not be traditional, but he has a lot to teach you if you'll listen and keep an open mind."

His head whirling, Gregg glanced briefly at Mac. Then he asked the Harrisons, "What did you learn? What did Mac tell you?"

"It wasn't just what he told us," Evan replied as he got up to refill his coffee cup. "It was how he showed us to use the tools in that old toolbox he carries on his shoulder."

Gregg was puzzled. "But…Mac told me he doesn't fix things."

"That's true," Graham said, nodding. "Mac doesn't fix objects. His tools and skills help fix businesses and the lives of the people associated with those businesses." He exchanged a look with his brother, who had gotten up to get more coffee. "Let's give Gregg an example of one of Mac's tools."

Taking his seat again, Evan asked, "Gregg, do you know what a life cycle is?"

Gregg felt a little disappointed. He associated this newfangled business term with a particular type of hokey, feel-good business speaker. He answered reluctantly, "Yeah, I think so. Isn't it the beginning and the end of something? How long a company is in existence, for instance?"

"Sort of." Evan took out a pen and began to draw on his napkin. "I'll show you." He turned the napkin so Gregg could see the drawing.

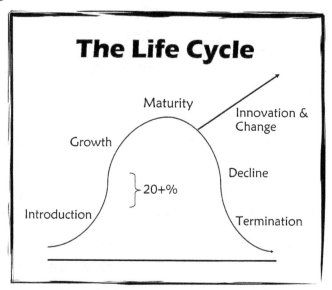

"As you can see here," Evan explained, "it starts with an introduction stage and then there's a growth period until maturity is reached. The next stages are decline and, finally, termination." Evan looked up at Gregg, who was studying the drawing doubtfully. "The important lesson we had to learn was to recognize and understand where we were—and are—on the life cycle. For example, a system that is no longer effective has reached the maturity stage, so it needs to be replaced or updated. On the other hand, a new product on the market is in the introduction stage. You can have all kinds of problematic issues arise, all at the same time, in various stages of the life cycle."

Gregg looked up from the napkin. "That seems logical, but… what's the point?" He tried to amend his borderline rudeness. "Your diagram made it easy to visualize the different stages, Evan, but I'm not sure I understand why the life cycle concept is so important."

Mac spoke up. "Gregg, in my travels, I have found that approximately twenty percent of the practices and concepts that businesses and organizations use to solve problems are not as effective today as when they were originally developed. Most companies have a difficult time weeding out which solutions are ineffective because the other eighty percent of the company is running well, and they tend to focus on the good majority instead of the bad minority. However, if they understood that all businesses follow the life cycle and that the laws of the life cycle always apply, they would be able to much more easily identify outdated concepts and replace them.

"Think of an ineffective system or obsolete procedure as an anchor," Mac continued. "An anchor's size is small in relationship to the boat, but that anchor can keep the boat from moving forward. Until the anchor is raised and stowed, the boat will make very little progress. At most, you'll just go around in circles. The same cause and effect happens in business practice. Unfortunately, instead of hauling up the anchor, so to speak, management often tries to just row harder in a fruitless attempt to forcibly propel the boat forward. You see examples of this in business when management wastefully applies more resources and energy to the same old, outdated solutions instead of removing them and creating new ones."

Gregg tried to keep his expression neutral as several "anchors" in his own business instantly came to mind. There were George Martin's shipping checklists, still on paper and clipboards, that the operations manager frequently misplaced; not to mention the damaged goods returns process, which basically consisted of items sitting in the warehouse until Gregg got fed up and packaged up a dozen or so, usually after hours. And certainly there were those stressful staff meetings. If they weren't anchors, Gregg didn't know what was.

Graham explained further. "In our case, we kept trying to address many of today's issues by using concepts that were twenty years old. For the most part we had a pretty good business, but it was not coming close to reaching its potential. From my banking background, I knew the numbers were weak. We had old debt and we were not in a position to leverage our purchasing. As a result, we missed too many deals that our vendors offered.

"Initially, it seemed that we had only mishandled one or two major things. However, as we spent more time with Mac, he helped us realize that there were profit leaks throughout our entire operation. The very first tool he pulled out of his toolbox was this wrench."

Evan reached into his desk drawer and held out the wrench for Gregg to see. Although he handled the tool with a great deal of reverence, Gregg had to hide his irritation. Here he had started to take this seriously, but the wrench Evan held was made of plastic and looked just like a toy, the kind found in tool sets made for kids.

But Mac had not missed his skepticism. "Gregg, I noticed that you enjoyed riding in my '46 pickup. That truck may have appeared unusual at first, just as this tool does right now, but give me some time. Things will become clearer as you begin to join the pieces together. Think of the action the wrench symbolizes rather than how it might normally be used."

Whenever Mac explained something it always seemed to make sense. Somewhat chagrined, Gregg thought, *I've put my disbelief on hold so far. Might as well see this through to the end.* He determined to give Evan his full attention as Evan began to speak.

"Gregg, the wrench reminds us each day to tighten the profit leaks that exist in each area of our company. Once we find the leaks, they are usually rather easy to stop. We learned how to identify these smaller leaks and stop them before they became a flood. We have actually increased operating profits twelve percent this year after an initial increase of thirty percent the previous year!"

Now that was what Gregg wanted to hear: numbers, proof, profits! He was not interested in a child's plastic wrench.

"With Mac coaching us," Evan continued, "we learned that many of these leaks resulted from numerous practices that we were still using, even though they had long ago become outdated in the life cycle—our anchors. The smaller leaks were basically ignored at first because some larger crisis would grab our attention and demand our time and energy.

"It didn't end there, either. Due to the fact that many different kinds of employees are involved in the activities that may cause a profit leak, we not only had to develop new ideas, we also had to make sure that our new ideas were implemented for the long term. We encouraged our employees to come up with innovative thoughts to improve our profitability, and then rewarded them for doing so. Any worthwhile new idea needed to stay in place long enough for the culture of the business to adapt to the changes and accept them into our daily operations."

Mac held up a hand. "Mind if I continue from here?" Mac turned to Gregg. "Employees are often your best resource for locating leaks. Since they are the ones closest to the details, they often have a perspective that you can't get as an owner and manager. So it's crucial that all employees feel as if they are a true part of the company—and that they feel empowered. Management must create an environment where no one is reluctant to identify areas that need improvement. Employees must feel free to bring their ideas to management. Too many managers and supervisors have a tendency to shoot the messenger. I'm sure you know what I mean by that."

Gregg shifted uncomfortably in his seat. He knew he was guilty of that very thing. But so many of his employees came up with such bad ideas, he justified.

Mac looked like he was resisting the urge to smile as he continued with his explanation. "Too often an employee will have a suggestion to improve a process or procedure that he or she is working on and is excited about. The supervisor too often perceives the message in a negative light. He or she doesn't listen to the employee in order to truly determine how the idea could impact operations. The supervisor sends the employee back to work, the employee is deflated, and any new ideas or thoughts from that person or his or her cohorts are cut off."

Gregg was frowning now. It felt like everyone was staring at him. Mac had described exactly how Gregg often treated his employees when they brought him what he considered bad news. It almost seemed like Mac and Graham and Evan had been spying on his daily operations and were now forcing him to own up to his errors. Well, it wasn't as if everyone didn't make the same mistakes as he did.

"I'm afraid I am guilty as charged." He tried to sound nonchalant in his response, but his voice had sounded a little more strained than he would have liked. He cleared his throat.

"Um...I have actually been told that it's not so much what I say that creates a problem but my body language and facial expressions. I think that sometimes people get the wrong idea about what I'm trying to say, but I'm not sure why that happens so often."

Mac nodded. "Gregg, you can begin to see how even small de-tails can cause shock waves throughout a business—and how improper communication can hamper understanding. It's true, as you have pointed out, that body language and facial expressions sometimes have a much stronger impact in the delivery of a message than the actual words being spoken."

Mac pointed to the wall behind Gregg. Turning in his seat, Gregg saw a small, wood-framed mirror hanging among various framed documents and photographs. Gregg realized that it was at a perfect height to be able to see his head and shoulders if he was sitting in the desk chair.

"I suggested to Evan and Gregg that they hang mirrors in their offices," Mac explained, "not to check their actual reflections but to remind them to try to see themselves as others might. I think that's a good idea for you as well. If you have the mirror's conscious reminder, it might help you to really listen to the feedback you receive from those around you. Keep an open mind and be grateful for the information that comes your way."

He paused, as if indicating to Gregg to listen extra carefully to what he was going to say next. "You first have to listen to understand before talking to be understood. Initially, it's important just to acknowledge the information you're given in a positive manner. You can decide its importance and area of relevance later. But encouraging employees to share information, regardless of its final value, will provide you with insight from people who have worked in a given area for months or years. Your employees are in the best positions to recognize problems and help stop profit leaks. You can't be everywhere every minute of the day. Encouraging and rewarding your employees will ensure that they continue to feed you valuable information. Just remember to use your mental mirror—and possibly your real one, too. It will work wonders."

Evan added, "With the information your employees bring you, you can determine where all your company's activities are along the curve of the life cycle without having to be constantly running around monitoring things. If you continue to waste money on concepts that have passed maturity and moved into the declining stage, you'll force your business into the termination stage."

Gregg held up a hand. "Wait a minute," he interjected. "I mean, I know this has happened in my company, but I can't understand how it *could* happen so often! You would think that someone would recognize these bad patterns and change the way they do business before they suffered any major losses."

Evan started to reply but Graham beat him to it.

"Let me give you a couple of examples of what happened to Evan and me. We assumed that if Dad had done something a certain way, then it must be the right way to do it. We tried to copy his style exactly and allowed past events to influence today's decision making. We were both in denial—big time. We felt that with my banking background and Evan's MBA, we were well equipped to take care of everything. And we had so much false confidence in ourselves, it convinced our advisors, employees, and customers to give more credit than they should have. They didn't question our efforts until it was almost too late. We were in conflicting stages of the life cycle. Product lines were maturing faster than we realized. We would hold on to them longer than we should and then have to sell them at discounted prices. That created significant profit leaks."

Mac gave Graham and Evan a funny smile as if they both knew what was coming next. Then he turned and spoke to Gregg.

"I have a wonderful investment opportunity for you."

Gregg suddenly wondered if this whole encounter had been some kind of elaborate sales pitch. He tensed and waited uncomfortably for Mac to continue.

"I know an automobile company that has discovered a new titanium alloy," Mac explained. "It's lightweight, strong, and rustproof. This same company has also patented a frictionless ball bearing that will dramatically increase wheel rotation and performance efficiency. Their Research and Development department has processed the leather for the interior so the luster will look new for twenty years. Does this sound like a potentially good investment?"

Sales pitch or not, Gregg was impressed. If this was their product, he was definitely intrigued. "Sounds good so far."

Evan grinned and took over the conversation. "The life expectancy of the halogen lights triples that of today's bulbs. Oh yes, they also have acquired the rights to a hydraulic suspension system that will provide the smoothest ride of all transportation."

Gregg was leaning forward now in his seat, listening intently. Was he going to be asked to buy a car? Then Mac added the last detail.

"Representatives of the company visited Kentucky's finest race horse breeding farms and selected a Thoroughbred with outstanding bloodlines and pedigree."

Gregg sat back in his seat slightly, not sure if he had heard correctly. "I'm sorry, but what does a horse have to do with the automobile company?"

Evan was the first to laugh. "They are going to design the latest and most technologically advanced buggy and hitch it to the finest Thoroughbred. The finished product will be the fastest horse and buggy to date. Now, how is that for a winning investment?"

Gregg sort of snickered, but he wasn't actually sure whether he wanted to laugh or felt angry for being taken in by the story.

Mac clarified the point. "The lesson is to recognize where you are on the life cycle. In the example we just gave you, all the technology is in the introductory and growth stages, while the idea or concept has long passed as a viable means of modern transportation. I have seen far too many companies apply modern technology and Research and Development dollars to a concept or idea that doesn't merit the investment."

Evan stood up. "If you come with us, we can show you what we mean." Graham followed suit, but Gregg hesitated, looking at Mac. Mac shrugged his shoulders, indicating that Gregg was to go ahead.

The two brothers headed with Gregg down the hall towards the back of the building, Mac following close behind. As they walked, Evan said, "We weren't watching our aging equipment and service trucks. Instead of rotating the trucks in our fleet when they reached the targeted mileage goals, we kept them past their projected trade-in values and took a big hit when they had to be replaced.

"We had discovered another profit leak," he continued. "We lost clients because our technicians were delayed by flat tires and overheated radiators. And we didn't have enough trucks to keep up with the amount of calls we were receiving."

Opening the door at the end of the hall, Evan said, "Now we have someone accountable for the fleet. This is a new position, one we hadn't realized we needed. Dad hadn't had one, so why should we? We were living in today's world but trying to think like Dad did back when he was our age. We should have known better because there were only six trucks back then, and now we have fifty-two."

They stepped outside into a parking area behind the building. Sure enough, dozens of gleaming company vehicles stood awaiting another workday.

Gregg felt a little bit sheepish. "I guess this is kind of like the software we were using until last year. Nobody upgraded it, and by the time we had to, the old software was so incompatible with the newest version that we had to enter the data manually all over again."

Graham shook his head sympathetically. "I think you're beginning to get the picture."

Mac put his hand on Gregg's shoulder. "We'll talk more about the life cycle later. For now, just try to understand how important it is to avoid wasting money on untimely ideas. He turned towards Graham and Evan. "I think we've taken up enough of your time today. Thanks for the coffee. It's great to see you two again."

They all shook hands, and then Gregg and Mac headed out front to the pickup. Gregg still wasn't sure what to think about this trip. He decided to ask Mac for some help.

"Mac, I'm not so sure I got all that much out of this experience. I'm still in a bit of a fog. It's early, I'm not quite awake, and all this still seems very strange to me."

Mac reached into his overalls pocket and retrieved a small spiral-bound notebook with lined pages. Then he reached into a side pocket and pulled out a stubby yellow pencil. He handed both to Gregg.

"Why don't you use these to write down the major observations you made, and we will review them together."

They climbed back into the pickup, and Mac drove while Gregg wrote:

notes

✓ Use the life cycle to identify the different stages of business systems and management styles, and make sure the stages are not conflicting.

✓ Beware of anchors-anything that keeps the company from moving forward.

✓ Don't address today's issues with yesterday's thinking.

✓ Stop profit leaks-they can create an outgoing flood. Remember the wrench.

✓ Don't shoot the messenger-make sure to encourage new ideas.

✓ Listen to understand before talking to be understood.

✓ Words may give one message, but body language and intonations often creates a stronger message, causing confusion.

✓ There can be no innovation without actual change.

✓ Use your mental mirror as a reminder to try to see yourself as others perceive you.

Chapter 3

After writing the last of his notes, Gregg settled back in the passenger seat and let out a long sigh. As the landscape flew by them, he finally had to admit it: this was no dream. Mac was real. The truck was real. As Gregg rolled the stubby yellow pencil between his finger and thumb, feeling its edges, Mac's voice brought him out of deep thought.

"Gregg, open the glove compartment."

Gregg leaned forward and punched open the small panel in front of him. He was astonished to see a computer screen inside the compartment.

"Now tap the screen with your finger," Mac instructed.

Gregg tapped the screen and the following image appeared:

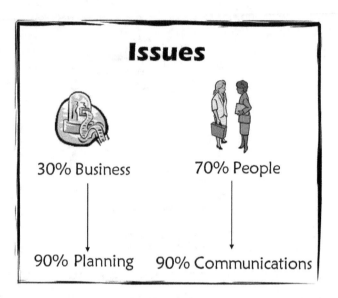

Mac talked as Gregg studied the diagram.

"Remember when we were discussing the issues businesses face in the life cycle? If you break them down, you will notice that only thirty percent of these issues are related to business."

Gregg gave Mac a dubious look, which Mac seemed to sense without taking his eyes off the road. He explained, "A business issue is something like deciding whether or not to expand into a new territory, or if you should add a new product. Other examples could be selecting how your company will finance growth or choosing to buy or lease equipment.

"The other seventy percent of your issues will be personnel issues. The majority of your effort will be spent figuring out how to handle employee issues—how you will motivate your staff and get them to perform at the desired level. The people issues take seventy percent of your time and energy; they are the problems that will wear you out by the end of the day."

Now that Mac had explained, Gregg motioned his head in total agreement. When was he going to learn to listen before making a judgment? "That actually sounds pretty accurate."

Mac gestured towards the glove box. "Look at the bottom of the screen. You can see that the majority of business issues result from inadequate planning, while the majority of personnel issues are caused by poor communication."

Gregg was beginning to get a little excited. It looked like the solution to his problems was pretty straightforward. "I get it now. Companies that plan effectively and efficiently and work on good communication will be more successful than those who don't. It seems simple enough, Mac. Those are pretty fundamental ideas."

Mac briefly gave Gregg an approving glance. "I believe you are starting to understand some of the real fundamental ideas of good business."

"Yeah, like the fundamentals of football—you know, blocking and tackling?"

"Well, sort of," Mac said. "The football itself is actually the fundamental of the game; you have to have a football before you can do any blocking or tackling."

Gregg was confused again and felt his impatience return. But before he could say anything, Mac continued.

"We assume when we explain something to another person that he or she knows exactly what we are trying to say. Often we assume that this person has a similar background or has had previous experiences similar to our own. We assume that they'll know exactly what we mean. Many times, though, things don't work out that way. Tap the screen again, Gregg."

Gregg tapped the screen like he'd rather punch it, and it instantly showed a new diagram.

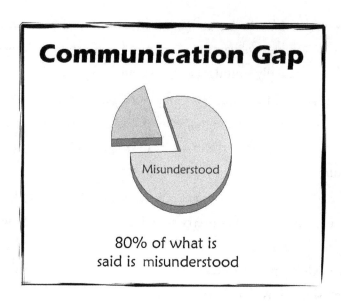

"Eighty percent?" Gregg scoffed. He couldn't believe that percentage was accurate.

"That's an average," Mac amended. "In some cases it's a little more, and in other situations it's less. The point is that ineffective verbal communication can disrupt any business or organization. Miscommunication can also take a toll on family life and social groups, of course, and it definitely impacts politics, as we all witness every day."

Mac pointed and said, "Tap the screen again."

A new diagram appeared and Gregg awaited Mac's next explanation.

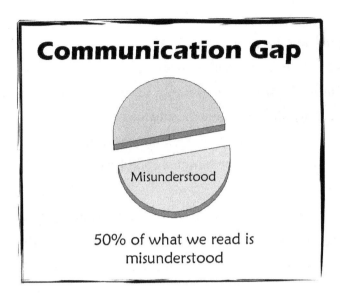

Communication Gap

Misunderstood

50% of what we read is
misunderstood

"The communication gap exists in our verbal communication and in our written communication. But by simply putting things into writing, it can help you to be better understood." Mac held up a finger. "But it is still important to make sure that any written messages also deliver a clear meaning that can be easily deciphered."

"Hang on a minute," Gregg protested. "I have been working with most of my staff for years. I don't need to write everything down for them. They should be able to understand my meaning by now just by my talking it over with them."

Mac exhaled slowly. "Really?" he asked. "Okay then...let's go back to last Monday's sales managers meeting. You asked one of the regional managers why the new product line was not achieving the sales goals projected at the beginning of the quarter."

Gregg felt a little unnerved by this comment. How in the world could Mac have known that?

"He told you that the line had not only reached sales goals, it had exceeded them. It took thirty minutes of everyone's time for the two of you to figure out that he was referring only to his territory. Part of the problem was that your VP of Sales, Mike, wasn't even at the meeting. If he had been, he might have figured out that you were actually interested in the total company's sales of the product line. There were six of you sitting in that meeting, so that discussion wasted three working hours of time. Multiply those three hours by the average salary of your staff, and that's what those wasted hours cost you. If it happened every week, you'd waste over one hundred and fifty hours a year."

It pretty much does happen every week, Gregg thought. He couldn't help but wonder how many similar misunderstandings had occurred.

Mac motioned for Gregg to tap the screen again. The next diagram clearly illustrated what he had been talking about.

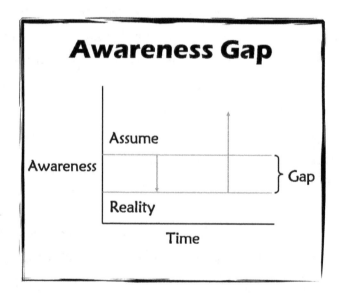

"Gregg, there is a communication gap and there is an awareness gap. Think about how incorrect assumptions affect productivity. For example, you assumed that total company sales for the new product were going to hit a certain figure. But this figure was dependent upon samples being delivered on time to the salespeople. In reality, most of the delivery dates from the vendors were delayed and the samples were not ready for all the salespeople. If you had looked at the situation from that vantage point, you would not have made your original assumption. It is true that one of your salesmen exceeded his goals for his territory. Now you know that his team had the samples and received their deliveries on time.

"If you look at the chart, you can see that the reality and assumption lines are parallel. They never meet. Think of the reality line as the productivity line in the example we just discussed. What you assumed—what you thought was taking place—is represented by the upper line on the chart. The difference between your assumption and the real picture creates what is called the assumption gap. To close that gap, you need to shift the assumption line down. Then you can look at the reality of the situation. You need to make sure that you have all the vital information instead of making assumptions. That's where encouraging your employees to come to you with problems and possible solutions come in handy. If even one of your regional managers had let you know that the samples were delayed, you could have adjusted your expectations, and you might have been able to call the vendors and move up the delivery of the order, or receive partial orders, or obtain the samples. You would have closed the gap and been more productive."

Gregg no longer felt like he was on a magic carpet; now he felt like he was riding a roller coaster. He'd gone from enthusiastic to confused to discouraged, and back to enthusiastic again, all within this short ride. He was discouraged by his understanding of how things could have been different. But the encouraging part was that he was also beginning to understand how things could be different in the future, if he made some fundamental changes.

With a half-hearted sigh, he said, "Okay, Mac. I guess I can give this a try at the office today."

Mac reached over and clapped Gregg on the shoulder in a gesture of encouragement. "I'm glad to hear it. But first, we're making another visit."

Gregg started to protest. He needed to get back home to finish getting ready for work and check on Elaine and his two daughters. However, when he looked at his watch, the time still read six fifteen a.m. He stared at the watch. Then he shook it and followed the second hand around several times. The minute hand remained stationary.

Feeling uneasy, he said, "Mac, I'm losing all account of time. This is not about me being impatient. This is about me feeling totally confused and more than a little freaked out."

"Don't get nervous, Gregg. I've got everything under control, including the time. Try to focus on the lessons. It will be a good use of time, and maybe it will help you calm down a little. Why don't you take out the notebook and pencil again and recap what you believe is important while I drive to our next appointment."

Resigning, Gregg flipped the notebook to a new page and started writing down highlights from his latest discussion with Mac.

notes

✓ Thirty percent of any company's issues relate to actual business processes; seventy percent involve personnel concerns.

✓ A successful business plan must be effectively and properly communicated throughout the organization.

✓ Blocking and tackling are not the most basic of fundamentals because to play at all, you first have to have a football-you have to know the game you are playing.

✓ Eighty percent of what is said is misunderstood, but only fifty percent of what is read is misunderstood. So write it down!

✓ Close the awareness gap, don't make assumptions, and break down the basics of communication until everyone understands what needs to be accomplished.

Chapter 4

This time, after he finished making his notes, Gregg leaned his head back against the seat. He was confused, intrigued, challenged, and mystified. He wanted to make sense of everything. If he could just close his eyes for a minute, all the pieces would start to come together and things would start to seem normal again. He had just started to relax when Mac's next comment startled him.

"We're heading to Greenville and we'll be there in just a few minutes."

Gregg's eyes flew open and he sat up straight. A trip to Greenville would normally take a little over three hours to complete.

"What's going on here, Mac? How are we almost to Greenville?" He held up his wrist and tapped his watch. "How is it still six fifteen?"

Mac just gave a mysterious smile, turning his head to briefly acknowledge Gregg before returning his eyes to the road. "Like I said, Gregg, you let me worry about the time. You have other things to think about."

At that point, Gregg decided he'd better stop trying to make sense of anything. Mac had said he would take care of things, and so far, he had. So Gregg closed his eyes again and settled back into his seat. When he felt Mac gently patting his shoulder to wake him, he realized he must have dozed off.

"We're here. I have some new friends for you to meet."

Mac had brought the truck to a stop near the entrance to a building. Lettered in a distinctive gold script, the sign outside read Douglas Law Offices—Attorneys-at-Law.

As they walked towards the entrance, Gregg noticed the nameplate on the front door. H. Douglas was identified as the Managing Partner, and S. Douglas and K. Douglas were partners.

"Mr. Douglas must have two fine sons," he commented. "Nice that they followed in his footsteps, isn't it?"

Mac paused for a moment. "You need to stop making assumptions before you know the whole picture. S. is for Stephanie and K. is for Kim—those are Harry Douglas' two daughters. Today they have a lucrative and prestigious law practice. It wasn't like that five years ago—but I will let them tell you their story."

They knocked on the door, and an attractive blonde woman dressed in a business suit opened it smiling. She gave Mac a quick kiss on the cheek and introduced herself to Gregg as Stephanie.

"Come on in. Dad and Kim are finishing up a brief, so they'll join us in just a little while. Please sit down and have a cup of coffee. I just made it, and you both look like you could use one." She was giving Gregg an appraising look.

Gregg was secretly wishing for something stronger than coffee at that moment, but he graciously accepted the mug from Stephanie.

"So..." she said to Gregg. "Mac chose you for one of his journeys. Are we your first stop of the day?"

Gregg swallowed his first of coffee. It was much better than the stuff he'd had with the Harrisons. "Um, no. You are number two on this trip. And I'm hoping that now the initial shock is beginning to wear off, maybe I will catch on a little more quickly."

Stephanie laughed out loud. "Don't worry, Gregg. I've been in your position, too, and everything turned out great." She turned to Mac. "Remember when Dad and Kim and I took one of your trips? It was almost five years ago."

Mac and Stephanie caught up as Gregg looked around at all the photographs of politicians, dignitaries, and celebrities. Among the collection was a photo of Randolph Tice, Governor of Tennessee, whom Gregg recognized from a TV interview he'd seen recently.

He was still staring at the photograph of the governor when Stephanie's father joined the group. "Harry Douglas," he said, introducing himself to Gregg. Then he noticed that the governor's photo had caught Gregg's attention.

"Randy is one of our favorite clients. The governor and I have known each other for over forty years. In fact we were roommates in college. I am proud to say that we strongly supported him in his reelection in Tennessee."

A cheery voice hollered out from some other room in the office.

"Brief is finished and ready to go, Dad!"

Kim's voice and demeanor were so jubilant, she almost seemed to dance into the room. She brightened the surroundings as she gregariously greeted Mac and Gregg. Gregg noticed how her short red hair and dark eyes contrasted with Harry and Stephanie's blond locks and blue eyes.

As soon as everyone was acquainted, Harry took charge.

"Sit down, everyone, and let's see what Mac has on his mind," he instructed in a deep baritone.

Mac smiled at his friends as they all took their seats.

"First, it's nice just to see the three of you. I also thought it would be helpful to Gregg if you could tell him how you transitioned out of the crisis environment that had been holding back your firm, and how you considerably grew your business as a result. I believe you told me you only had to add one clerical position and an additional paralegal to handle the increased workload."

Harry looked thoughtfully at Mac, and then turned to Gregg. He was a tall man, even sitting down, and he had an air of shrewd intelligence. However, his voice, when he spoke, was warm and inviting.

"As a quick background—I was a widowed father working my way through law school while trying to raise these two beautiful daughters." Harry smiled briefly at both Stephanie and Kim. "Once I passed the bar, I joined a large firm as an associate and helped prepare cases for trial. One day, I had the opportunity to try a small tort case, and remarkably, I won it! I was so inexperienced that I didn't realize I had been opposing a lawyer with outstanding credentials. To me, he seemed only to be interested in finishing the trial as soon as possible. I was probably overly prepared, as it was one of my first cases. Anyway, he got away from the basic law, tried to ad lib as he argued the case, and lost on a technicality. That gave me the exposure I needed. I began to work my way up in the firm. When I became a partner, Stephanie was clerking for Judge Waring, and Kim had entered law school."

Kim interjected her side of the story.

"I always loved animals and I wanted to be a veterinarian, but I decided it would be in my best interests to join the family firm."

Harry patted his daughter's shoulder, clearly used to her impulsiveness. "After a few years, Stephanie joined me, and then Kim came on board. Since then, the firm has grown and grown. That's the good news. The bad news is that we grew so fast that we didn't have time to plan or to become well-organized...."

Kim seemed unable to keep from interrupting her father as she chimed in again. "Dad, it wasn't that we didn't have the time to plan. We didn't make the time to plan."

Stephanie seemed to have decided that she might as well put her two cents in at this point, considering that her sister had no qualms about it.

"We were always putting out fires, Gregg. We had no focus, so any direction we took seemed okay. We overcommitted, so as much as we wanted to be responsive lawyers, we often kept our clients waiting."

Stephanie only got those few words out before her father spoke up again.

"What made things worse was that communication between the three of us was horrible." He chuckled, remembering. "As you can see, our office space is not that large. We are never more than fifty feet apart, and yet six years ago the left hand didn't know what the right hand was doing. We were being redundant in our efforts so that we often duplicated each other's work in preparing for trial. We even went so far as to do the paralegal's work, so she was unhappy and looking around for anything to fill her time. We were so engrossed in our cases that if she asked a question or needed to know how to perform a new task, we usually just brushed her off and did the job ourselves. I remember thinking that in the time it would take me to show her how to do a particular job, I could do it myself."

Kim suddenly jumped out of her seat. "Dad, let's grab the charts that Mac gave us and show them to Gregg."

She opened the doors to a wall unit, unrolled three charts and pinned them to the corkboard. Harry stood to join her, and before she could cut in again, he began to explain the diagram on the first chart to Gregg.

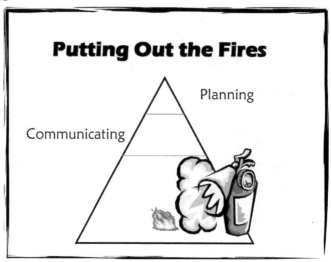

Putting Out the Fires

Planning

Communicating

"In this first illustration, the triangle represents a time unit—it could be a day, week, or month. The top of the triangle indicates how much time the three of us spent planning our practice six years ago. You can see that it accounted for very little of our time. The second section illustrates the only slightly larger amount of time we spent communicating with each other. Yes, we talked about cases and our practice in general, but the discussions were limited and occurred sporadically. Unfortunately, the remainder of the triangle reveals where we spent the majority of our time: putting out fires that we mostly created ourselves."

"We were operating in a total crisis environment!" Kim broke in excitedly. Stephanie put a calming hand on her sister's arm, and Harry continued his explanation.

"We hadn't figured out that it would have been better to take the extra time to do things right the first time, and we kept making excuses for why we hadn't done so from the beginning. Yet we seemed to accept that we had to take extra time later on to correct everything we'd done wrong initially. It was pretty ridiculous, actually, since correcting our mistakes took up much more time than just having a planning meeting in the first place."

Mac sat up straighter and raised a finger in the air. "I have a great example of that. I made a visit to a building contractor some years ago. In one of our discussions he gave me a hypothetical example that simply explains the issues here. He said that if he built a segment of a job and it wasn't done correctly, he would have to repair that section, which usually ran to four times the cost of the original work. He always enjoyed telling me that time had the same value as money. What he meant was that if actions are done right the first time in a given time unit, then four time units can be saved by not having to spend extra time, energy, and money on costly repairs or corrections."

He turned to Gregg. "The lesson is this—time is money. When you are operating in a crisis environment, you spend too much of your time putting out fires. This type of company environment or culture is the result of zero planning and a lack of focus. Being reactive instead of proactive is not productive; the inefficiency costs time and money, and it limits growth."

Kim had remained quiet and still as long as she could.

"It seemed we were always picking at one another. We would snap at each other because we were working long nights and still never had enough time to prepare for a trial. I would go home exhausted and frustrated. That was the way we conducted our practice for a long time. After a while, it became habit. We grew so accustomed to this business lifestyle that we didn't notice how negative we were being towards each other."

Stephanie interrupted her sister without apology, rising from her chair. Gregg was beginning to see how these three might have had some trouble communicating.

"It kept getting worse, Gregg," Stephanie said. "Instead of putting out the fires, we added fuel to them because of the way we conducted our day-to-day activities."

Walking over to the visual display, she pointed to the next chart and continued with her explanation.

"This second diagram indicates how, even in a small office like ours, we set each other up for failure. The figure at the top is giving instructions to the figure below, and as the arrow indicates, there is movement back up to the top figure. I have a perfect example of this.

"There were times I would go straight to our paralegal and tell her I needed research to be done on a particular case. Most of the time I was stressed out, so I usually wouldn't give her all the information she needed to do the research. So, of course, Ellie, the paralegal, would walk into my office a little bit later with a legitimate question. Instead of helping her with the answer, I'd grab the file and tell her I'd do it myself. I didn't give her the chance to learn and I definitely didn't take the time to train her. Instead, I gave her the impression that whenever she had a question or didn't know how to perform a certain task, I'd just handle the situation myself."

Mac glanced at Gregg, glad to see that his newest protégé was really paying attention. "Have you ever heard of the monkey theory?" Seeing Gregg shake his head, he continued, "It takes place when an associate has a monkey on his or her back, so to speak, and that associate comes to you with the problem. When he or she leaves your office, you now have the monkey on your back. At the end of the day those monkeys—those problems—can be a very heavy burden. This is called upward delegation, and by allowing it, you reinforce that kind of employee behavior. If you always do the task or solve the problem for your associate, he or she will not learn to address their own issues and…so goes the circle as you see on the chart."

Harry joined the conversation again, gesturing to the chart.

"Look on the left side of the illustration. The figure with the question marks represents an individual who has been left out of the loop. In business, this is usually a middle manager or a supervisor. In our case, it was always one of us. I'll give you an example that occurred in our firm. On this chart, I am now represented by the top figure on the phone, and the paralegal is the figure you see at the bottom. I'd ask Ellie to check on a title for a piece of property. When I didn't receive the information I'd requested, I'd then ask Kim why Ellie didn't have it ready."

Kim let out a soft laugh, but her father continued undeterred.

"Kim would have no idea what I was even talking about, and she'd just get annoyed with me and go back to her own work. That would make me angry, so I'd lash out, which I seldom do. But Kim couldn't have known what I wanted. It took a little while for me to understand what had actually transpired, but when I fully realized what had gone wrong, it had a profound effect on me. This one incident was only the tip of the iceberg; it was one of many symptoms that were signs of the poor procedure we had developed. I was inundated with work, and since I wasn't using Ellie in an efficient manner, there was no relief for me. That was my issue. By not planning anything and then always scrambling to beat the clock, and by not communicating well with Stephanie and Kim, I was paying a heavy price. I was constantly adding fuel to the fires."

"It was at this point that Mac entered our lives," Stephanie said, her eyes filling with warmth as she looked at the carpenter. "We were in our conference room late one evening, working and eating take-out Chinese. I knocked over a container and it spilled all over a stack of important papers. I let out a series of cuss words that I knew Dad had never known me to use. Right then, Mac walked in with a roll of paper towels and started to clean up the mess. Trust me when I tell you that our initial reaction to Mac was probably the same reaction you had, Gregg."

Her comment made Gregg relax a little. At least it seemed that those meeting Mac for the first time had once felt weird about him materializing seemingly out of thin air.

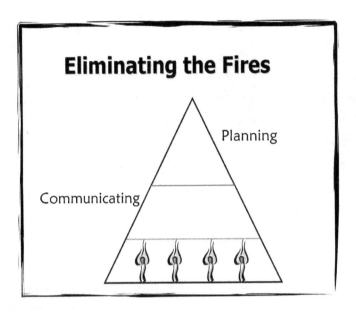

"Mac's visit was the defining point for turning the practice around," Harry agreed. "See, the next diagram of the triangle has changed considerably. The upper line is now lower, indicating that the three of us are spending more time planning our practice. At first, we didn't want to take the time to sit and plan things out. But with Mac's help, we realized we had two choices—learn to efficiently run the firm, or waste time putting out fires. We chose to make improvements. This major change also taught us to communicate effectively with each other. Even though we're all in the same family, each one of us still speaks our own unique language. I'm sure Mac will explain that to you later, in greater detail."

He returned to the table and sat down. "The three of us learned that with better planning and communication, many of the fires just disappeared, pretty much for good! The triangle itself has not changed, only what's taking place within it. By pushing each section's line down— or, in practice, by spending more time planning and communicating— there's less room in our day for fires. And it's the reoccurring problems that are the most disastrous; they have the greatest impact on an organization. Things like always being late for a hearing or having incomplete legal research or failing to delegate to our paralegal are just a few examples. Sure, there will always be some unavoidable emergencies like a judge being called away from the case or additional evidence coming in at the very last minute; but now when these unavoidable events happen, we have the time and energy to devote to manage them."

Mac quietly stood up after Harry finished this last explanation. Looking at his pocket watch, he motioned for Gregg to stand also.

"It was so nice to see you all, but it's time we head on. Thank you for taking the time to share your experiences with Gregg."

Turning to the two Douglas daughters, Mac gave each one a hug goodbye and then shook Harry's hand. As Harry and his two daughters walked them towards the reception room, Kim slipped her arm through Gregg's and whispered a secret in his ear.

"I've always had the feeling that Mac somehow caused Stephanie to knock over the Chinese food on purpose, just to make it seem like he had a legitimate reason for helping out. He not only helped us clean up that spill, he helped us clean up the big messes that were cluttering up our lives. I cannot tell you how much this one event fixed not only our practice, but our personal lives as well. I don't have to spend as much time away from my family, and now when I'm at home, I can truly enjoy my time with them. I have time for all the important people in my life and I'm really enjoying everything more."

Her whispered words made Gregg envious, and he realized for the first time that this might be his chance to regain some control over his business and especially his life.

He and Mac hopped back into the truck, and as Mac put it into gear, Gregg automatically picked up the notepad and stubby yellow pencil and started to write down what he had learned during his second visit of the morning.

notes

- √ Operating in a crisis environment means you will spend too much time and energy putting out fires.

- √ Learn to eliminate the fires before they ignite. Take the time to do things right the first time.

- √ Don't add fuel to the fires: devote ample time to planning and proper communication.

- √ Learn to be proactive, not reactive.

- √ Don't be a victim of the monkey theory; eliminate upward delegation.

- √ Use the chain of command to communicate.

- √ Learn how to delegate properly.

Chapter 5

As Mac pulled out of the parking lot, Gregg felt like his brain was overflowing with new information. "What did Harry mean when he said that even though they're in the same family, each one of them still speaks their own unique language?"

Without taking his eyes off the road, Mac said, "I was wondering if you were going to ask that question. As you learned from the Douglass, planning and good communication are important ingredients for a successful business. Gregg, do you realize people usually spend more time planning for and talking about an upcoming party or vacation than they spend on planning their businesses?

Gregg couldn't help a snort of disbelief. "That can't be true."

Mac raised his eyebrows. "You don't think so? Think back to last month when you planned your daughter's party."

Gregg's eyes lit up at the mention of Cristina's party. "Yeah... what a blast! We had a great time and it came off without a hitch."

He had blurted out his reply before it dawned on him that, once again, Mac somehow knew all the intimate details of his life, both professional and personal.

Quickly, he continued, "I'm tellin' you…um, well it sounds like you already know…but anyway, it was quite an event! Everyone really seemed to enjoy the party. Elaine and I watched Cristina's reaction all during that evening and we could tell that all of her dreams had come true."

Mac smiled at Gregg's exuberance. "Now, Gregg, describe the sales managers meeting you held last week."

Gregg scowled. "Come on, Mac. You've already given me one example of how badly it went. By now, I get that you probably already know it was a complete disaster or you wouldn't have brought it up."

Mac wasn't giving up. "Well, why did it turn out to be such a disaster?"

Gregg sighed impatiently. "Well, first of all, Nancy, my secretary, messed up the reservations at the facility. She didn't reserve enough rooms for all of the sales team members that were coming in for the event. My PowerPoint presentation was rushed because I waited until the last minute and missed emphasizing the main points I wanted to deliver."

"Anything else?"

Gregg fumed. "You already know what else went wrong! The agendas were misprinted! The new samples were late again! The point-of-sale information didn't arrive! Just about everything that could go wrong did go wrong. You are only adding salt to the wound. I thought you were supposed to fix lives, not tear them down further." He crossed his arms, somewhat petulantly.

Oddly, Mac was trying to suppress laughter.

"If your daughter were here right now, I think she would tell you to chill out. I am here to help you fix your life, and to help you make a positive impact on the lives of others. But if we don't have a few reference points to go by, you will never fully experience the benefits of managing differently. It's not so much that you've been doing everything wrong. You really just need to manage differently. Remember what we discussed with Evan—the idea of anchors that can keep you from moving forward? Which events acted as anchors and held the sales meeting from moving forward like you envisioned?"

Mac's questions really made Gregg stop and think. He wasn't exactly sure why everything had gone haywire at the meeting. His interest was piqued, but he wasn't sure he could stand to hear what Mac had to say.

Finally letting out a low whistle. "Okay, Mac. I'm ready for the sermon."

Mac frowned at the sarcastic remark.

"No sermons here. I know you don't see me as a preacher, because I certainly don't look like one. I dress the way that I do because it is easily recognizable and nonthreatening. It helps folks relax and identify with me. You see, I do fix lives, not objects like a regular carpenter. I fix lives by being a mentor, a coach, and a confidant. I am not here to judge. I'm just here to tell you what I've observed. So I can also be a sounding board for you, and for the others who have accompanied me on my trips. I'm not here to give lectures or preach sermons."

Gregg just listened. He felt bad for making it seem like he wasn't taking Mac seriously.

Mac continued on with his explanation. "The tools I have shown you so far are meant to act as reminders of the changes you should consider making in your own life. Think about how you should change your management style: how you delegate, how you plan, and how well you communicate those plans to others. These changes have to be your idea. I will help you uncover some of the issues that you need to work on, but you must own up to these issues; and the recommendations, changes, and solutions must be yours. Don't think of me as an outsider telling you how to run your business. Think of me as your partner. I consider your success to be my success. But the final decisions are yours and yours alone."

It seemed to Gregg that Mac was the one with all the good ideas. "Why are you putting so much emphasis on the fact that these changes need to be my idea?"

"Because if they are yours, that makes you their owner. And as an owner you are far more likely to hold onto them, so they will have a long-lasting value."

Seeing that Gregg was still baffled, Mac tried another approach. "We talked about using the football as a symbol for returning to the purest of basics in business and life. Think about this. Have you ever wondered why people don't do what you ask them to do?"

Gregg thought for a moment. "I guess it's because they don't know how...or maybe they don't understand what to do, or where to get started...or maybe..." He ran out of ideas.

"No, no, no, Gregg. Hang on a minute. You're making this point far too complicated. If you ask someone to do a task and they don't do it, the reason is simply that they don't want to. That's getting down to the pure basics. That's the football. If they really wanted to do what you've asked them to do, they would find ways to learn or understand. They would seek out any method necessary to accomplish the goal. The lesson to be learned is that you have to influence others to *want* to perform or change. But don't forget that it starts with you, and you have to 'want to' first."

Gregg thought about all the things he hated to do around the house—empty the garbage, repair the fence, the typical chores. He was always putting them off. But things like washing and waxing his Mercedes, or helping Elaine landscape the yard, he enjoyed; and he did them as often as he had time. And even though he hated running errands, he was always happy to drop Cristina off at a friend's house simply to spend time with her.

He hesitated before asking another question, feeling that Mac must be wondering how anyone as clueless as him could have run a business for more than twenty years. But he wanted to understand. He wanted things to change. Finally, he asked, "How do I make someone want to do something they don't want to do?"

Instead of being irritated, Mac seemed pleased that Gregg had asked the question. "When someone recognizes a problem or an issue they become the owner of that issue. In other words Gregg, it's theirs" he answered. "The same is true when someone comes up with a recommendation, or a solution. Since they thought of it they want to solve an issue using their own recommendations. Typically, people "want to" see their ideas be successful. There is not as much desire when the idea comes from someone else."

"What do you mean, issues?" The question came out before Gregg could stop it.

Mac was thoughtful for a moment. Then he said, "Think about it like this. You have a headache, and you take a couple of aspirins. Four hours later, when your headache comes back, you take two more pills. You are trying to cure a symptom. You are not curing the issue or problem that is actually causing the headache in the first place." He glanced over at Gregg, who indicated he was following.

"Have you ever thought about curing the cause of the headache and eliminating the need for repeated medication?" Mac continued. "In this example, the headache is a symptom and the root cause of the headache is an issue. Most people are only interested in getting rid of the pain as quickly as possible. They keep popping aspirins, hoping for immediate relief. Those who try to ward off the same headache for years will just experience the same pain over and over if they continue to only address the symptoms."

Gregg threw up his hands. "How do I know if I am dealing with the symptoms of a headache or its root cause? How can I be sure I'm addressing the real issue?"

Mac, as ever, remained calm. "Take a look at some common examples. During my visits, many of my friends ask me to help them increase their sales, profits, productivity, morale, or ROTI. They also want to find ways to reduce expenses, overhead or debt."

Gregg held up his hand and interrupted. "Hold on, Mac, before you go any further—what in the world is a roti?"

Mac couldn't resist the urge to tease Gregg a little.

"Don't tell me you've never heard of ROTI! ROTI is one of the top three concerns of most businesspeople. I'm pretty sure that I'm correct in saying that it's your number one priority. How could it be so important to you, and yet, you say that you don't even know the meaning?"

Gregg rolled his eyes but couldn't suppress a brief chuckle. "Mac, just stop messing around with me and answer my question, please."

Mac grinned. "Just trying to make sure you're still paying attention."

"I'm all ears. So tell me."

"ROTI stands for return-on-time-investment."

Gregg just stared. "That's all it is? How could that be my top priority?"

"You told me earlier that you worked long hours and often weekends. You complained about not spending enough time with your family. When you increase your ROTI, you will spend less hours working and have more time for your other priorities. Now does it sound pretty important?"

Gregg responded sheepishly. "Yes." When Mac was silent, he asked, "So how do I increase my ROTI?"

Mac smiled. "It all starts with awareness of how you use your time. Being aware of how you spend your time in your business and in your life is key."

"Umm…that's really not much of an answer, Mac."

"Gregg, why do you try to complicate everything?" Mac said while laughing. "You have to remember the football! The basics are not running and passing; the purest of basics start with first figuring out which game you are playing. Knowing that you are playing football and not rugby is vital information to have before you plan to begin coaching even the fundamentals of running and passing. How many successful football coaches gained their experience playing rugby? Both sports have passing and running, but the most basic of fundamentals for each game are different—starting with the ball."

Mac continued as Gregg slowly started to nod his head in understanding. "The same is true with time. It's one commodity that cannot be replaced—once used, it is gone forever. When time isn't used properly, there's no return on the time expended. When you use time wisely, you increase your return on your time invested. With that in mind, let's go back and compare Christina's party with the sales meeting."

Gregg felt his exasperation return. "Why are we back to that again?"

"This is important, Gregg, or I wouldn't bring it up again." All humor was now gone from Mac's voice. "Why did Cristina's party go smoothly? What happened to cause the sales meeting not to go as you would have liked?"

Gregg put his head in his hands for a moment, let out an exaggerated sigh, and thought about each event.

"In the first place, I don't think it's fair to compare a girl's sixteenth birthday party to a sales meeting. Because…the party was fun to plan, and business has no place for fun. You're asking me to compare apples and oranges."

Mac gave Gregg an unamused look that made him squirm a little.

"You know what I mean, Mac," he tried to explain. "Parties involve guests and friends and music and food. Business is work—it's not supposed to be fun. Fun versus no fun. Fun is always going to come out on top!"

"Why can't business be fun, Gregg?"

"It's work. That pretty much says it all, doesn't it? You go to work and work. You go home and relax, or go golfing, or you travel—now that's fun."

Mac was silent for a moment. Then he said, "Why can't you make work include fun, just like those other activities in the other areas of your life…like with parties for your daughter, or golfing, or tennis? There's work involved in organizing a party, or in practicing your golf game so you can improve. So if there's work involved in fun, why can't there be fun involved in work?"

Gregg was speechless. Mac might as well have asked him why they didn't continue their conversation in Chinese. He was about to retort, but then he started thinking about what Mac was suggesting.

Finally he burst out in a laugh. "What a novel idea!"

"It's not new, Gregg. Many people incorporate a lot of fun elements into their careers every day. My philosophy is that business can be fun. I have proven it too many times to count. When your journey is over, you'll have a better understanding of how to make your business fun and how to turn work into an enjoyable and rewarding experience. But unless you want to make the journey, it won't do you much good."

Gregg still doubted that this philosophy would hold up in the reality of his business world. In truth, however, he hoped he could learn to make his business as fun as his personal life. When he thought about it, that was what he had always wanted. It would be a whole new way of experiencing business life—and that would make his personal life better, too.

"Okay, I'm beginning to see the relevance of all of this," he said. "Let's go back and compare the party to the sales meeting, as you suggested."

Mac looked pleased. "All right, then. Besides having fun preparing for the party and not having any fun with the sales event, in what other ways did they differ?"

Gregg thought for a moment, frowning. "I don't know. In both cases, I took charge of the planning. With both the party and the sales meeting, I told everyone what I wanted and what they should be doing. I prepared for both events. The difference was that everyone involved with the party did as I asked and things ran smoothly. Just about no one involved in the sales meeting did what they were supposed to do."

Mac gave a very slight sigh, but his tone, when he spoke again, was far from impatient.

"Gregg, indulge me a little more. Let's go back and recount exactly what you told the VP of Sales and your secretary."

Gregg looked out the window at the blurry landscape. Briefly he wondered where they were traveling next, and if he really wanted to go there. Half of him wanted to tell Mac to take him home. But he answered Mac's question.

"I told my secretary to reserve an appropriate location for the meeting and to reserve the hotel rooms, compose my PowerPoint, and create an agenda."

"Did you tell her how many rooms she would need, or if the rooms and the meeting location should be in the same hotel?"

Gregg thought for a moment. "Well, no, but that just stands to reason…I mean, she knows how many sales team members we have."

"How about the samples and the point-of-sale information? What happened with all of that?"

"I guess I told Mike what he needed to know…I can't exactly remember, but I'm sure I did that. And even if I didn't, he should have known anyway. He's been around long enough to know what to do. That's what I pay him good money for. I shouldn't have to hold his hand at this point."

"Okay, then. What happened when you saw the preparation falling apart? You must have noticed it going astray at some point during the planning process."

"I did what I always have to do. I quit everything else I was working on and took over the planning for the meeting."

"In other words, you took the places of your sales VP and your secretary?"

"Well, what else was I supposed to do?" Gregg gave an exasperated shrug. "There were thirty-five salespeople coming in and they had to have a place to stay. I was trying to avoid total chaos. Neither Mike nor Nancy seemed to be able to find the right kind of place to hold the meeting. In the end, I just called my club and got a room without much trouble. And if I had just done the agenda myself and checked on the samples and POS information, there wouldn't have been any blunders there either." His tone had grown sarcastic again.

"Well, Gregg, do you feel you got a good return on your time invested in preparing for the sales meeting?"

"Hell no!" Gregg snarled. Then he blinked, surprised by his own vehemence.

Mac, however, was unfazed. "Well, why not?" he asked. "Why was your time wasted?"

"Because every time something really needs to get done or a deadline is looming, everything always falls back on me. Haven't you heard the phrase, *the buck stops here?*"

Mac nodded. "I've heard it before. So let me make sure I've got this straight. You did all the tasks that the VP of Sales and your secretary should have done, but they still received their paychecks...I'm assuming. They didn't both decide to hand their pay over to you, did they? I imagine not. Didn't you have anything else to do with your time besides bail them out of trouble?"

Gregg was just about done. He rolled his eyes and let his breath out in a huff. "Okay. Let's stop the Q and A for a while, can we? Just tell me what you are driving at and let's move on with the show."

"This Q and A, as you call it, is how I coach. I want you to see what the true issues are. I don't want you getting them confused with the symptoms. If, by self-discovery, you can uncover or diagnose the problem and come up with viable solutions, then you will be the owner of both the issue and the solution. Understand?"

"You know, at this point, I don't want to be an owner! Just give me two aspirins to get rid of this splitting headache you've given me."

Gregg tried to laugh a little to let Mac know he was partly kidding, but Mac didn't seem amused at all.

"Take out the notepad and pencil and write down these questions," he said.

Gregg muttered under his breath again, but Mac just ignored him. He dictated and Gregg wrote:

1. Did you have a planning meeting with your VP of Sales and secretary like you did with the caterer, florist, and stationary salesperson?

2. Did you inform your secretary of the specific types of facilities you wanted, or tell her about the availability of the club, or discuss the budget for the rooms?

3. Did you emphasize to your secretary the salient message you wanted to make in your PowerPoint presentation?

4. Was there enough time for you to proofread the agenda?

5. Who was accountable for contacting the vendors for the samples and point-of-sale information?

Gregg stared at the list on the notepad and exhaled his frustrations. He gazed off into the distance for a moment. His temples were really throbbing now, but the desire to argue had gone out of him. Once again, Mac was right.

"Okay, Mac. I see. I haven't been noticing the important issues. So…how about we start fixing my life right now?"

Mac reached across the truck's cab, put a hand on Gregg's shoulder, and spoke in a very kind tone.

"I started to do that the moment you chose to climb into my pickup and go on this journey. I told you that I fix lives, but I never said it was an easy thing to do. Changing the way you conduct your business starts with being aware of your present behavior style and the impact it has on everything you do. The two main essentials you need to lock into your brain are these: you need to improve your planning process, and you need to improve your communication skills. Understand, not everyone runs their personal lives and business lives the same way. Most of the time, one area is given preferential treatment over the other. You told me earlier that your business is important to you—that it is your very livelihood—and yet, compared to the sales meeting, you handled the party far more efficiently and with much greater enthusiasm. The only way you were able to pay for your daughter's party was with earnings you made from your business. Wouldn't it make sense, then, that you should give your best effort to your business plans, too?"

Gregg groaned. "Mac, I'm sorry for being short with you. I wanted you to just give me the answers and let me get back to my life. I think I get it now. I have to be aware of exactly what's taking place in my business life if I ever want to become more efficient and effective." He looked down at the notebook in his lap. "I feel like I used to be better about my business matters, but over the years, things seem to have gotten away from me."

"Think back to when you first opened," Mac suggested. "Who was in charge of sales, operations, and finance?"

"I was. There was no one else when I first started the company. I had been a sales rep and had always wanted to start my own business. I had an opportunity to buy out a sales rep that represented four lines in two southern states. In the beginning, I was the chief cook and bottle washer."

"Then what happened?"

Gregg was starting to get animated again. "I worked my butt off, that's what. I knew everything that was taking place. As the business grew, I formed a company, hired a sales manager—the same one we were just discussing who's now VP of Sales. Later on, I added an operations manager and then promoted the bookkeeper to controller. Today, we have fifteen diversified lines that we represent throughout the Southeast."

The thought of how he had made his business grow over the years brought a slight grin of satisfaction to Gregg's face. Despite his recent problems, he realized that he had managed to do some things right.

Mac's question brought him back to the present. "But as the business grew and you began adding personnel, you lost your alignment. Is that right?"

"Alignment? What are you talking about?"

"When you were the only chief in your company, you were accountable for everything. When you made a decision in the sales area, you knew how it would impact operations and finance. However, this only worked while the business was relatively small. Back then it was easy to have a comprehensive view. You had the sales, operations, and finance circles aligned in your head. You understood how they overlapped—how they related to each other. I'll show you what I mean. Open up the glove box and tap the screen."

Gregg popped it open and tapped the screen. A diagram illustrated the concept that Mac had begun to describe.

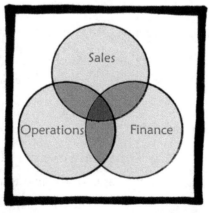

"As you can see," Mac continued, "the three circles overlap each other. When you hired the sales manager, he took the sales circle with him. Later, the same thing happened when you hired the operations manager, and then with the promotion of the controller. The sales manager was doing what you had told him to do, which was to go out and make as many sales calls as possible. I bet his job description hasn't changed since his promotion to VP of Sales, just his salary. The operations manager was made responsible for the warehouse. His job was to supervise receiving and shipping. To him, you emphasized the importance of watching expenses and keeping overtime down. Then you told the controller to make sure to pay the bills and keep the bank off your back."

"Yeah, that's pretty much what I told them. What's wrong with any of that?"

"Let's take a look at all the pieces. Analyze the circumstances and see if anything seems amiss. I'll coach you if you get stuck."

Trying to determine which part could have had any problem areas, Gregg started by telling Mac about each member on his management team.

"Mike, my VP of Sales, is a fireball. He started out as a sales rep himself, and he can sell ice to Eskimos. When I turned him loose, our sales took a gigantic leap upward. George over in operations had the warehouse humming and got everything done without going into overtime. Sally kept the bank and vendors off my back, just like I had asked."

"Sounds like a good team, Gregg. How did they all get along?"

"Well…everything was just fine, at first. Things ran smoothly. But as soon as some major problem came up, they'd all start blaming one another for everything. No one really took responsibility for any of the mistakes that occurred. That part drove me crazy—probably drove them crazy, too."

"Give me an example of a major mess-up," Mac prodded.

Gregg thought back. "Well...Mike was always busy pushing product, but often he would cut the price just to make a sale. This would send Sally up the wall because it reduced our margins and lessened the cash flow that was needed to pay the bills and the bank. Mike would also make commitments for George and shipping. We had designated cut-off times to ship out orders, but Mike kept abusing the cut-offs to please customers. As a result, George started to incur extra overtime. Sally would then complain to George because the additional costs were affecting her cash flow. I can remember, one time, I walked into the break room and they were about to kill each other. I literally had to step in and break Mike and George apart."

"That sounds pretty rough. Let's take a closer look at what really was transpiring. Did Mike have any margin goals? Was his compensation based on sales or the margins between what you paid for the product and what he sold it for?"

"Umm...no, no margin goals for Mike. He only focused on getting sales and didn't give consideration to actual profits. He was and is still paid a flat salary plus a bonus."

"What's the bonus based on?"

"If the company does okay, I pay everyone a bonus; and if we don't do well, no one receives one. I would think that's pretty standard."

Mac frowned, but moved on. "Back to the alignment of the circles...Mike had his circle and it was not aligned with George's or Sally's. George's main focus was to keep down the overhead, which did not align with Mike's sales goal of selling as much product as possible and keeping customers satisfied. Sally's mission in life was to pay the bills and satisfy the bank. She was not involved in customer service or staffing in the warehouse. She was primarily interested in daily deposits.

"The fighting in the break room occurred because of all the finger-pointing. Because your business had outgrown the operations structure and management style, there was little time for planning and little effective communication. The culture quickly became reactive. A reactive culture creates crisis and turf wars. Everyone involved in the clash actually blamed the others, and each fought to protect only the circle that had been assigned to him or her."

Gregg shook his head at the mess he'd created. "I had no idea. That certainly was not my intent."

"I know that," Mac reassured him. "When you dealt with the caterer, florist, and the other folks involved with the party, they clearly knew your expectations. You held them accountable for their performance. They knew that if they did not meet your expectations, they would never have you as a client again; and worse yet, you might tell other people around town that their performance was shoddy.

"You said earlier that the preparations seemed perfectly choreographed and everything flowed along effortlessly. This was accomplished because you planned everything in great detail—not because you got involved with the details after everything was already in chaos. Your communication was effective so that everyone knew their role, knew how they should communicate with the other participants, and knew when tasks needed to be completed. You created a winning combination."

He gestured to the notepad in Gregg's lap. "Look at the questions you wrote. Now can you see the difference between the two events?"

Gregg could feel his indignation rising again. "Mac, I pay an excellent salary and bonus to the sales VP. Nancy, my secretary, is also in the top of her pay range. They should—"

Mac interrupted before Gregg went off in the wrong direction again.

"What if you'd called the florist and said you needed flowers for your daughter's party, and then just expected her to pick out something you'd like? What if you'd done the same thing with the caterer? What if you'd just told the calligrapher the date and time of the party—how would she have known you wanted more information on the invitations?"

That stopped Gregg in his tracks.

Mac continued. "You gave the vendors all the information they needed to pull off the event successfully. You didn't expect them to know what you specifically wanted just because it was their job to provide flowers and food. But you expected that of your staff. Because you were paying them, you expected them to read your mind. But how could your secretary know that you'd made changes to the PowerPoint if you didn't tell her? How could she know about the availability of the club without your communication?"

"That was dumb, wasn't it?" Gregg admitted. "I guess I've been expecting everyone to do what I would do without them knowing what exactly that was."

Mac shrugged. "Everyone makes mistakes. The trick is to learn from those mistakes. You are a very bright person. You're just in need of a little redirection."

Gregg looked away for a few minutes. He needed a moment of quiet. Watching the scenery fly by in a blurred flash made him a little dizzy, however, so he turned back to his chauffeur.

"Hey, Mac, where are we going now?"

Mac looked straight ahead and replied in a loud, grand tone, "To the Tower of Babel! Andrew Jenkins can tell you all about people who speak different languages and how that can make working together more difficult."

Gregg rolled his eyes. "That's all I need now—a Bible lesson."

Mac laughed out loud. "Gregg, take out the pad and pencil again and jot down what you've just learned. You don't have a whole lot of time. We'll be there in two shakes of a lamb's tail."

Gregg opened the pad and began to write.

notes

- ✓ People do not do what is asked of them when they have no personal desire to fulfill the request.

- ✓ You have to influence others to want to change but you have to want to first.

- ✓ You must be the owner of and accountable for your issues and their solutions.

- ✓ Cure the issue-don't just treat the symptom. Aspirin is not the answer.

- ✓ Improve the return on time investment (ROTI).

- ✓ Learn how to make business fun.

- ✓ Improve planning and communication skills to move from a reactive to a proactive workplace

- ✓ Align the circles and make sure they stay connected after you've given them to others to manage.

- ✓ Remember that the activity in one circle often impacts the activities of other circles.

Chapter 6

As Mac slowed the pickup to what seemed like a normal speed, Gregg's thoughts were a kaleidoscope of images. He was starting to understand the points Mac was making, and damn if they hadn't begun to make sense.

Looking around as Mac motioned him out of the truck, he had no idea of his location. Mac had called this place "the Tower of Babel," but the only object remotely resembling a skyscraper was a smoke stack located behind an enormous manufacturing facility. There was a great deal of activity; a shift appeared to be changing, with workers coming and going.

As they approached the entrance a deep, friendly voice rang out and a giant of a man approached them. "Yo, Mac! What's up, my main man? So good to see you, now come give me a big hug."

Mac did as he was told and was grasped in a bear hug.

The bear-hugger immediately turned his attention to Gregg. "Who's your friend? Don't tell me he's on one of your 'visits.'" He reached out and engulfed Gregg's hand in his large, callused one. Gregg felt like a small child shaking hands with an adult.

"Andrew Jenkins," the towering African-American said, beaming at Gregg. "Drew to my friends. And if you're a friend of Mac's, you're a friend of mine."

Feeling somewhat overwhelmed, but undoubtedly welcomed, Gregg introduced himself. "Gregg Herbert, glad to meet you."

Drew beckoned them inside with a wave of his arm. "Mac, Gregg, come on in. As you can see, the shifts are changing and it's a little chaotic, but things will simmer down soon and I'll show you around."

They entered an ultra modern reception area with photographs of oversized earthmoving equipment. Gregg noticed a wall of citations and awards earned by the company, along with an impressive assortment of testimonials, before he was swept along into an Employees Only area. They proceeded through a maze of offices that were both orderly and striking—minimalist, Gregg conjured as he took in the décor.

At the end of a corridor the three entered an oversized office with a desk and furnishings to match. Drew asked Mac and Gregg to sit down and took his own seat behind the massive partner's desk. As he settled in, his bulk transformed the surroundings to a proportional size.

As usual, Mac initiated the conversation. "Drew, why don't you give Gregg some of your background."

Drew grinned, something Gregg figured he did a lot. "I can do better than that. I'll give you some highlights of my bio—but I know the real reason Mac brought you here, and I will gladly cover that as well. It's one of my favorite subjects."

He settled back in his chair. "I was born in a rural farming community in South Carolina, the oldest of six siblings. My mama loved to read to all of us, and I was the first in my family to attend college.

With my grades and football experience I received a full scholarship to the university."

Something clicked in Gregg's mind. "Weren't you known as 'The Crusher'?" There had been considerable state pride in the young athlete, which Gregg could remember from his high school days.

Drew once again treated him to a flash of teeth. "I see you keep up with sports. I'm impressed that you remember so long ago. Yeah, that was my sports page name, but frankly I would have preferred to be remembered as graduating with honors and being recognized as a scholar-athlete. Back then the headlines sold more papers screaming about "The Crusher" winning a game or making a play than mentioning that I received an A in accounting or unofficially tutored the other players."

Gregg was still astonished to be in the presence of a would-have-been football great. "You got drafted by the New York Jets out of college, right?"

"And won Rookie of the Year in my league. Unfortunately—or fortunately, as it turns out—I tore my ACL in my right knee and hung up the cleats the end of my third year with the Jets."

Gregg glanced over at Mac, who was sitting quietly with his arms folded, apparently enjoying Drew's enthusiastic storytelling. Turning back to Drew, Gregg ventured, "You say 'fortunately.' I assume that's because of all this…." He gestured at the room around them.

Drew nodded. "I was able to continue my education and received an MBA from Wharton using my signing bonus. Then I was hired by Southeastern Manufacturing as a management trainee. I've been here for a little over thirty years. Guess you could say this is my second home."

Mac picked up the conversation. "What Drew isn't telling you is that he became a sales exec in short order and soon was selected to service only the national accounts. He exceeded all sales records and was appointed VP of Marketing. From there he was elected President by the board and today he is Chairman and CEO."

Gregg leaned back in his seat, studying Drew. If anyone looked like a chairman and CEO, it was not Drew Jenkins. Besides his stature, he was dressed in a Polo shirt, neatly pressed khakis, and Docksiders.

Drew was shaking his head good-naturedly. "What Mac isn't telling you is that becoming president was when I really got into trouble. Then along he came to my rescue."

"Mac seems to have a knack for rescuing others," Gregg admitted. "Why did you need rescuing? How did he come into your life?"

"It was about six months after becoming president. I was taking the job seriously—too seriously. I had always gotten along well with all kinds of different people in most levels of business. I had great fun with my co-workers. My direct reports liked me and knew they had my support. When I was VP, Mr. Walker, 'The Prez,' as we referred to him, kept telling me he was grooming me for his job.

"He did just that and I was grateful for his trust and confidence. But as soon as the president title followed my name and all the employees knew my new position, there was a shutdown."

"Shutdown?" Gregg asked.

Drew nodded. "It seemed to me that no one wanted to talk to me. In fact, I thought no one wanted to have anything to do with me. When I discussed this with Marge, my wife, she pointed out that I had changed. She said I didn't listen to any of my family anymore and that my body language gave every indication to stay away from me.

"I was pretty shocked, but I started thinking about what she'd said. It was true; I was short with her and the kids. Soon I noticed that other people, especially those I worked closely with, weren't grasping what I was saying. It was like we were all speaking different languages. Kinda like the Tower of Babel."

Gregg cut his eyes at Mac, who gave him a quick wink as Drew continued.

"I was sitting in my office late one night trying to piece together what had happened. I was looking at a photo of Marge and the kids and praying for an answer to tell me what to do. It was exactly at that moment that I felt another presence in the office, and when I swiveled around there was Mac sitting across the desk with his toolbox resting on his lap." Drew gave a brief laugh. "Gregg, I thought I'd lost my mind."

"I know what you mean," Gregg muttered.

"Drew had the answers to his dilemmas inside of him," Mac interjected. "He just needed a little coaching to figure out what the issues were and how to go about solving them."

"I know," Gregg responded. "He had to own his issues and their solutions."

At this, Mac and Drew both gave each other a high-five.

Gregg looked back and forth between them. "Don't hold me in suspense any longer! What were Drew's issues?

"Intimidation, for starters," Drew answered. "As you may have noticed, I am not a small person and I have a deep voice that can be intimidating to many people. Add a frown and staccato remarks while pushing people for answers before they are ready added fuel to the fire.

"Even at home Marge would be all over my case. 'Slow down. What do you mean? I don't understand what you are saying! Speak to me in terms I can comprehend!' It's a good thing I married her—even at five-four and a hundred and five pounds she can get my attention."

Gregg thought briefly of Elaine. His wife rarely commented on his business, but over the years they had worked out a system of communication that usually did the job...at least, that was what he thought. Elaine and his daughters were important to him, and he hoped their communication was better than it had been in Drew's family. He made a mental note to follow up. *Wouldn't do much good if I got the business straightened out and my family life fell apart.*

Drew continued, "I tried desperately to be understood and speak in simple terms, but it didn't help. Then I was accused of putting others down or belittling them. My performance was suffering, and so was my staff's. That was one hell of a way to run a company."

Baffled, Gregg asked, "So what happened?"

Drew grinned devilishly and opened his desk drawer, retrieving a small object. "This, this is what happened." He tossed a small plastic yellow disk sander to Gregg.

Gregg caught it easily. By now he no longer expected to understand, so he turned to Mac and joked, "Oh, I see, this makes perfect sense." With the toy sander held high in his hand, he continued in a grandiose manner, "Do you care to explain the meaning so that I may be enlightened?"

Winking, Mac asked, "Don't you remember the 'tools' I gave out in our previous visits? This is another one, and it is to be used as a reminder of what issues you should be resolving."

"And how does this disk sander resolve intimidation?"

"Not so much intimidation. This sander is a reminder of using the DiSC."

Gregg appealed to Drew. "Was Mac this obscure with you? I mean, you have to work for every little thing!"

Drew grew serious. "Yes, Gregg, he was. And I was just as impatient as you are. I was at the end of my rope, and I needed answers—now. But think about it this way. Do you want Mac to hand you everything on a silver platter? That'll solve your problems temporarily. But you said it yourself—you've got to own your issues. If you don't, you'll just have to deal with them again as soon as Mac is gone, and it won't be in the right way."

Somewhat chastised, Gregg looked down at his lap.

"Think about it, man," Drew urged. "I mean, this isn't even taking a day out of your life!"

Gregg was startled into looking at his watch, which still read six fifteen a.m., even though he was feeling more like lunch than breakfast at this point. Turning to Mac, he spread his hands. "All right. The disc. What is it?"

"The DiSC is an acronym for the four basic behavior styles we all have." Reaching into his toolbox Mac pulled out a small PDA and asked Gregg to flip open the lid and touch the screen. When he did, Gregg read:

D   DOMINANCE

I   INFLUENCE

S   STEADINESS

C   CONSCIENTIOUSNESS

Mac explained, "These are the words that describe the four basic behavior styles we all possess. Each person differs in behavior due to the intensity and importance of the four in their makeup."

Drew took up the explanation. "I am sure Mac has told you that eighty percent of what we say is misunderstood and fifty percent of what we read is misinterpreted."

"Yeah, and if you want to improve communications thirty percent, just write it down," Gregg acknowledged. "So let's get to it!"

"Gregg, I swear you must have been taking lessons from me," Drew said with a big grin. "I believe we were both born under the same sign, and that sign is a big **D**."

Gregg waited. Although he had no idea what Drew was talking about, he was somewhat comforted by the fact that this successful CEO had something in common with him.

"I was overly conscience of my size," Drew went on, "and so I made it a point to keep others at ease and disregard their rude remarks. But when I was elected president, my priorities changed. I made it a mental note to do the best job I could for the company and for me. I was going to take the previous efforts and successes of Southeastern Manufacturing and make them even better. In my enthusiasm and hard drive, the intensity of my **D** behavior rose and drove people away.

"I'm sure Mac has impressed upon you by now that the most important resource of any organization is its people. Think about it from an accounting standpoint. Most of the long-term assets on your balance sheet are either depreciated or amortized. The long-term asset that you want to grow is your people, and they will grow only if they want to. I had lost the idea of getting their 'want to's.' I was dominating, not mentoring or coaching."

Gregg thought back to a conversation he'd had with Mike just the week before. He realized that part of the reason work was no fun was because he'd started to feel like he had to boss his employees around just to get them to do anything. Not that it was working.

Drew continued, "You cannot take your employees for granted. They need to feel special, feel like they're needed; and they need to receive recognition when they accomplish something. Compliments are a must, but I fell into the trap I have seen too many managers fall into: believing that if employees are told they are doing a good job, they will quit working as hard. That is complete rubbish. I had a line coach in high school who always found fault with everything. No one could please him, ever. When he had to relocate, the team said their thanks for his departure. The next season, the new coach instilled in us the importance of teamwork and how each one of us was making a contribution to the team. He found ways to correct us in what he termed a 'sandwich.'"

"Speaking of sandwiches, I'm starved," announced Gregg. He had a feeling they were going to be here a while, and he always listened better on a full stomach.

Drew broke into laughter and glanced at Mac, who raised his hands helplessly.

"We should be able to come up with something from the cafeteria." Drew made a call for some refreshments, and soon an assortment of sandwiches was delivered. Once Gregg had his plate, Drew continued.

"Now, listen and think about what's going into your head instead of your stomach." When Drew had Gregg's full attention he continued. "A sandwich is a wonderful method of correction. You say something positive, then make the correction, then compose another positive statement at the end. You sandwich the correction in between two compliments. The coach's sandwiches worked so well we had the best record the whole time I was playing. We went on to win our conference championship, but I have always said we weren't the champions; it was that coach."

Putting his plate on the table next to him, Gregg sat up enthusiastically.

Drew leaned forward over his desk and folded his hands. "Mac has been my coach since we first met. I've learned from him the importance of understanding the communication and awareness gaps, and especially not to assume what others say. A wonderful gift he gave me was to learn to listen with three ears."

Gregg swallowed, wondering if by the end of the day he'd be speaking in riddles just like Mac and now, apparently, Drew. "Come on, Drew, we only have two."

"Yes, Gregg, and in your case God gave you two ears and one mouth, so use them in the correct proportion."

Chagrined, Gregg made up his mind to soak in Drew's words of wisdom.

Drew ticked off on his fingers. "The three ears consist of:

"The first ear—hearing what someone is actually saying;

"The second ear—understanding what an individual does not want to say; they may not want to discuss a particular topic.

"The third and most important one—what someone does not know how to say. He may not know how to express himself or is intimidated by the conversation."

Gregg thought to himself, *I can see it now. Mac will reach into his toolbox and pull out a hearing aid for me.* He was beginning to think he could use it. He kept telling himself to listen, but for some reason he kept fighting Mac. It wasn't logical.

While no hearing aid was in evidence, Drew's explanation did seem to somehow improve Gregg's hearing. As Drew explained how he had returned to his original philosophy in dealing with employees and worked on his sensitivity, each word seemed to contain extraordinary clarity.

Finally, Drew brought it all together. "Part of my understanding how to be sensitive to others comes from the DiSC. I am only going to give you a quick overview, but I will give you all the contact information for you to become proficient using the DiSC as a communication tool."

He printed out a couple of pages and then handed Gregg a box containing the sanding disks. Upon closer examination Gregg saw a **D, I, S,** or **C** clearly printed on each disk.

"Disks come in different coarseness and are selected and applied for different sanding tasks," Drew explained. "One isn't better than the other, as they are all equally important when used properly. But, just as with any tool you have to be careful when and how you use it. For instance, if you use the coarse one for a polishing job you get into serious trouble."

"It's like when I play golf," Gregg spouted out, and then hesitated. Here he was complaining about not getting an explanation, and he wouldn't let Drew finish. "Sorry, I didn't mean to interrupt."

"Quite the contrary, let's hear what you have to say," Drew replied.

Mac had turned in his seat to acknowledge Gregg straight on, which made Gregg feel a little nervous, but he plowed ahead. "I was having an awful time controlling my driver on the golf course. I would either slice or hook, and I never knew where the ball would land. Hey, isn't that interesting. The driver starts with a **D**, and **I** was using High **D** behavior." He grinned.

"That's one way to remember it," agreed Mac.

Gregg held up the sander with a **D** on it. "The letter **D** in the DiSC stands for dominance, right? I was trying to dominate the fairways and it totally ruined my scores. It took me a long time to figure that out. I would fume and fuss and take out my frustrations on the others playing with me. I felt bad, and I know they must have wanted to throw me into the nearest pond like I did one day with my driver."

"What happened?" Mac inquired.

Gregg shrugged to show the simplicity of his solution. "I started using my three wood and began to hit the balls straighter. I didn't get the distance, but my score improved dramatically. So…is changing clubs like changing letters?" he asked, sincerely wanting to know.

"You don't necessarily replace one letter with another the way you do with clubs," Drew said, "but if your High **D** behavior is not working for you then it needs to be softened, or used less, and the other letters emphasized. In my case I was an off-the-chart **D** to the point the other letters had near zero value."

Gregg continued his investigation. "So then how do the letters work?"

"The higher the intensity of each letter, the more it comes into play during your communications," Drew explained. "As we have been discussing, my **D** was too high. I needed to strengthen my I letter. Remember, **I** stands for influence, and influence is a wonderful way to approach others in any situation. The high **D** behavior is task oriented, while the high **I** is oriented towards people. You have to have both, but I was focusing too much on getting the job accomplished and not enough time on the folks doing the work."

He spread his hands wide, an admissive gesture. "Gregg, I was born a **D**. That is my primary behavior or core behavior style. I will never lose it, but if I can mix the **D** behavior with the **I** behavior, I can have a winning combination. There are other combinations of letters that are just as successful in communicating with others. It's knowing how to mix and match the different behavior styles that makes for effective communication.

"That is what attracted me to Marge," he reflected, smiling indulgently. "You know they say opposites attract. Besides being the prettiest girl in my class and a cheerleader, Marge has a High **I** behavior profile. At the time I didn't know one letter from the other, but I did know Marge was a fun and energetic person who loved people. She treasured being the center of attention. She verbalized well, was a great persuader, and always had something funny to say to cheer me up. I guess you can say her High **I** behavior and being a cheerleader went hand in pompom." He laughed. "That was a **D** trying to make a joke—hand in glove. Marge's traits are the key tendencies of **I** behavior."

"So what about the **S** and the **C**?" Gregg held up the S sander and toyed with it. "How do those fit in?

"The **S** behavior style, steadiness, is one that wants to cooperate with others to carry out a given task," Drew answered. "High **S**'s like dealing with repetitive types of work and have a much higher level of patience. **S**'s want to be accepted by the group they are in and want to keep things pretty much the same. In other words, they do not like change. But if change comes along, they have to be given plenty of time to make that change. It's also important to **S**'s that they know how things are to be done. They are great listeners and wonderful team players. They are exceptional when it comes to following through, which is a big help in any company.

"**S**'s need to be invited to participate." Drew thought for a moment. "The best illustration for that is Sharon, one of my best employees. I was having our annual planning meeting with my staff. This is an important gathering because our strategic plan and budget are derived from this and similar meetings. After we were into our discussions for well over an hour, I noticed Sharon sitting at the end of our conference table with her hands folded and head down. I wasn't sure she was even listening when I asked her if she would like to add anything to the conversation. Without picking up her head she elaborated for twenty minutes about the plan and gave a great deal of input for budgeting. We were so impressed with her input that we called the plan Sharon's Strategic Initiative.

"What is so interesting about Sharon is that she's a single mother of three teenage daughters. And I'm telling you, her girls toed the line, made all A's and were active in their church. I kept thinking that Sharon could not be an **S** at home; she had to be in charge. Then I realized that while she is an **S** at work, at home she is a **D**. These two letters are as far apart as two behavior styles can be. I became fascinated with Sharon's two behaviors. How could one person be so different at work and at home?

"The two of us had discussions about her behavior and I learned Sharon thought her place in our business was to be a **S**, so she was going to be the best **S** she could be. But when the staff gave her permission to be a **D**, her whole demeanor changed. She elevated her **D** behavior style and lowered her **S** style. She simply changed the intensity of these two letters. Now she's in charge of several committees and has played a viable role in our company. The lesson, Gregg, is that sometimes you have to give **S**'s permission to be a different behavior style, if that is what they need to be, and invite them to participate."

Gregg sat back in his chair. "So any of the letters can combine in a successful way? I mean, **D** and **I, D** and **C, S** and **C,** and **I** and **S?**"

"Once you're aware what you are, then yeah, you can tone it down and emphasize another way to communicate," Drew said. "Now, **C's** are the analytical people. They have to know everything there is before they can make a decision. They need a great deal of information and truly weigh the pros and cons. They are great planners and are systematic in their approach to a problem. **C's** are cautious and pay close attention to standards. Our CFO is a **C,** and that behavior style fits him to a tee. But sometimes he drives me crazy when it takes so long for him to give me an answer. **D's,** like me, want answers quickly. Sometimes my behavior style is 'ready, fire, aim' while Jimmy's is 'ready, aim, aim, aim.' Between the two of us we balance our behavior effectively."

He paused, as if offering Gregg the opportunity to ask a question, but Gregg simply waited, listening, so he continued. "I had to learn that different behavior styles are okay. My staff didn't have to communicate the way I did. As I learned more about accepting the different styles, I was better prepared to create an effective team. I had to learn that it is imperative to recognize the different behavior styles and respond to each one in the appropriate manner."

"Well, I think I can certainly relate to that," Gregg muttered almost under his breath.

Mac gave a chuckle and Drew grinned as he wrapped up. "Let's get back to where I started—how things fell apart after my election. I didn't know one thing then about the DiSC. All the examples I gave you were after Mac gave me the plastic sanders and spent what seemed like an inordinate amount of time explaining its subtleties. But, as Mac puts it, it was in the briefest of moments.

"In trying to live up to my expectations of the job, I pushed the C's for answers long before they were ready to give them to me. I wanted to know the bottom line—what's it going to cost, when will we get the raw materials, how much will the proposed procedure save? I didn't know that **C's** processed information differently than I did, or that they communicated at a different pace. Before Mac, I had it in my head that everyone communicated like me and that was it!"

Gregg could easily see the similarities between Drew and himself. He was fascinated when he compared himself to Drew. They had such different backgrounds, were involved in completely unrelated businesses and circumstances, and yet their behavior patterns were almost identical. What had he stumbled upon? *Am I starting to see the light?* he thought to himself.

Shaking his head, he turned to Mac and said, "I appreciate your patience with me. I have been so stubborn."

Mac reached out and placed a friendly hand on his shoulder. "No, Gregg. You're just in need of a little coaching to help you see reality and not assume so much. You need to understand behavior and motives and learn to hear with your three ears. You do some of these some of the time, more so in your personal life. You need to do more of them most of the time. I'm not asking you to be perfect. None of us are. I want you to understand the bare basics—the football of life and business."

Gregg finally had to ask. With all the references to football, he had been wondering for a while. "Mac, what do you compare business to when you're helping women?"

Both Mac and Drew glanced at each other. "Drew was actually the one that originally brought up the idea about business and football, kind of like you did," Mac admitted. "And usually my female 'clients' do fine with it. A game is a game, after all. Kim Douglas did make a point to come up with a tennis metaphor; she said it wasn't geared towards men or women, so it would be more politically correct. You should ask her about it sometime."

Gregg thought that particular exchange might take a while.

Drew stood up. "Let's go, fellas. I'll show you around. Put on these visitor badges and we'll go out and watch progress at work."

Overall, Gregg was impressed with the company. The manufacturing process was well executed, but what he was most struck by was Drew's involvement with his employees. He seemed to know not only their names but their families' names as well, and he asked them about everything from their vegetable gardens to the purchase of a new car. He pointed this out to Drew.

"I couldn't have done it without Mac," Drew explained. "He's helped me to build a team—and I mean a team—that works well and communicates effectively. All our letters have blended. And I'm able to recognize each person as a gift and work to develop him or her to their fullest potential."

Several of the employees paused in their work to wave as the three passed. Drew clapped one of them on the back.

"Sam," he said, "tell Gregg here how much of an improvement we've seen since Mac showed up."

Sam wiped his brow and grinned up at Drew. Jabbing his thumb into Drew's chest, he said, "I like him a lot better now than when he first took over!"

Drew and Sam shared a laugh at this, but Gregg found himself suddenly wondering what people were saying about him as a boss. Reluctantly he admitted to himself that most of it probably wasn't complimentary.

After the tour Mac and Gregg said their goodbyes. As they headed to the truck, Gregg felt as if a weight had been lifted from his shoulders. He felt a calmness he had never experienced before. He couldn't explain it, but he knew it had something to do with Mac.

"You know, Mac," he said as they climbed in, "I need to tell you how excited I am since I first met you in my bathroom and began this trip. I am really looking forward to seeing how all this will work for me. I just hope I'll be able to remember everything."

Mac had paused as he started up the truck and turned to look at Gregg. Now he said, "I'm glad to hear it, Gregg. And don't worry about remembering; you'll have your personal tools to remind you."

Then he put the truck into gear and they drove away. As Gregg was writing his observations he was struck by the fact that the pencil always remained sharp but didn't become shorter as if it had been in a pencil sharpener. Fascinating! He jotted down his thoughts.

notes

- √ Give corrective criticism using the "sandwich" concept.

- √ Listen with three ears.

- √ Understand and use the DiSC: dominance, influence, steadiness, consciousness.

- √ Learn to balance the four letters to improve communications.

- √ Remember that everyone does not communicate in the same manner.

- √ Don't forget-people are the most important asset of an organization.

Chapter 7

Gregg was finally beginning to look forward to his next "visit" with Mac. "Where to this time?"

Mac's answer surprised him, to say the least. "Atlanta."

Gregg was a little dismayed, as Atlanta was over three hours away, but he remembered the ease with which they had reached Greenville. Plus the sense of calm he had gotten after visiting Drew was still with him. He felt his back press against the seat of the truck much the same as it did when a plane took off. As the pressure released, he glanced out the window; again the "view" was a complete distortion.

Feeling the notebook in his shirt pocket made him glad to know he would have his reviews with Mac available for future reference. Still, he had mixed emotions. On one hand he was excited about trying out the new concepts; on the other, he wasn't sure he could pull it off as the Harrisons and the Douglas had done. He wasn't losing confidence; it was just all so new to him. He wanted to change; he wanted to "own" his issues and their solutions. He wanted his business to be fun and enjoyable! *And I am going to give Mac my full attention for the remainder of this trip*, Gregg promised himself.

As Mac slowed down and the view came into focus, Gregg realized they were in an upscale suburban area. Mac pulled into a boutique plaza filled with specialty shops, and the pickup came to a stop in front of Ashley's Fine Stationery. As they exited the truck, Gregg was immediately attracted to the window display with its variety of paper products and writing instruments.

It was still too early for the store to be open, but Mac rang the bell and a woman in her thirties looked up and dropped what she was doing. When she saw Mac, she ran to the front door. Mac was embraced lovingly, as a daughter would with her father after a long absence.

"Jennifer, meet Gregg Herbert. Gregg, this is Jennifer Ashley."

Jennifer greeted Gregg and pulled Mac into the shop by his hand. Gregg followed, amused at the continuously enthusiastic reception Mac always seemed to receive. Jennifer's shop was elegant and professional in its design with an air of refinement and comfort; although Gregg could tell its products were expensive, it was not stuffy or intimidating; nor was it cluttered.

Jennifer had just finished brewing a pot of coffee and offered them some in bone china cups complete with saucer. Gregg could not remember when he had had so many cups of coffee before breakfast but took his, enjoying the vanilla aroma. Watching her catch up with Mac, he noticed that Jennifer was outfitted in a designer suit with matching accessories, and she exuded such personality. Gregg felt at ease even in these unfamiliar surroundings.

As if reading his mind, she turned to him and said with a big smile, "Welcome to my world of pens and paper."

"This is quite a departure from earth moving equipment," Gregg laughed, noticing her striking green eyes. He was also comparing Drew's bulk with this petite woman. "Mac, you are not going to tell me that

Jennifer and Drew have similar backgrounds and issues. I know she wasn't an offensive tackle for the Jets."

Mac tried hard to conceal his amusement. "Yes and no," he replied. "Yes, there are many of the same issues, and no, the backgrounds are night and day. But remember, Gregg: when dealing with people, all the issues are essentially the same, only in varying degrees."

He turned to the woman beside him. "Jennifer, tell Gregg how you started this business."

Jennifer cut her eyes to the side mischievously. Gregg could tell she had told this story before. "I love to be with people and I enjoy selling. While I was raising a family, my husband traveled a great deal and I was looking for an outlet. I woke up one day with this idea of selling custom designed stationery from my home. I did some research and found access to a few of the boutique lines and sold them to my friends. I had no business experience but as long as I sold them for more than they cost I made a few extra dollars."

Gregg could not tell if she was joking or this was the truth.

She continued, "My little business grew, and more and more customers began asking for more choices. But there was only so much room on the dining room table, so I was torn between keeping the business at home and opening a shop. The idea of opening a real business terrified me! I didn't know the first thing about running or managing one. I knew I had good product lines, but I had no idea where to open or even if I should."

Sipping her coffee she continued. "On day I was playing tennis with my tennis partner, Jordyn Hannon, and she said she wanted something productive to do with her extra time. Her children were older than mine and she had more free time than me. That sparked off months of discussion until we finally decided to open a shop near our neighborhood. There was a small space for lease in a strip center, and since it was convenient for us we made the plunge.

"The business did okay because we were located near our friends and most of the new customers coming in we already knew. However, there wasn't enough volume to pay for the overhead. Fortunately, we had subleased the store and only had a year's lease. That first year we realized there are three essentials to making a profit—and they are location, location, location." She held up a three fingers to emphasize her point. "We also learned not to select the inventory *we* liked; we had to choose what our customers wanted. It quickly became apparent they did not always have the taste we did, so we had to run sales to give the slower moving inventory away. I learned later from Mac that that was a 'profit leak.'" She glanced briefly at the gray-haired carpenter, who indicated for her to go on.

"We had this checkbook mentality—as long as there was some cash in the account we would be okay. But it kept running out before all the bills were paid, and so we had to supplement the business from our personal funds.

"A friend of my husband is an accountant. Daniel Stevens volunteered to come over and take a look at our books. He had been in public accounting but recently opened a small practice with his brother. I hated to tell him the only 'books' we had was our checkbook." She laughed ruefully.

"I will fast forward my story by saying Daniel straightened us out and we saw our financial picture for the first time. We took the time he spent with us seriously, as we were receiving an accounting course in short order. Since then I've been amazed how many entrepreneurs don't understand the finances of their own businesses."

As Jennifer stopped to catch her breath, Gregg thought about his last three year-end financials from his CPA were in his desk drawer in unopened envelopes. He had been too busy to listen to the pleas of his accountant to discuss them. All Jimmy wanted to talk about were the same issues his banker friend, Don, wanted to discuss at their lunch scheduled for today. *Maybe now is the time for me to take a hard look at the financial end of my business*, he thought reluctantly.

Facing Gregg Jennifer continued, "Our best advertising is word of mouth, so that has been the basis of our success. We began to understand our customers and what they wanted from us both in product and services. We heard over and over again that they actually enjoyed spending time with us. So we decided to start serving coffee and offering cookies. But as Jordyn was pouring a cup for a customer selecting wedding invitations, she realized the paper cup did not go with the surroundings. We realized how important it was to not only meet our customers' expectations, but to exceed them and create 'raving fans.' So we bought these bone china cups and saucers, and they turned out to be just the ticket. Gourmet coffee replaced the common brand, and we began to use real cream instead of the powdered stuff. To my surprise, no one volunteered that this was an improvement—but all the customers obviously were enjoying drinking the coffee and munching on French pastries.

"One day I decided to ask a regular how she liked the refreshments. She told me, 'Jennifer, besides visiting your wonderful shop, the coffee in the morning or the tea in the afternoons brightens my day. It is always a pleasure to sit down, relax, and be treated like I am important, instead of some clerk doing me a favor to wait on me.' She told me it was so disheartening to walk into a store and be imposed upon by 'May I help you?' Her standard answer was, 'No thanks, just looking.' She mentioned this to her husband, who's a business professor at the university. He told her that this kind of retailing is combative; that when she is greeted in that manner she has been preconditioned to answer the way she does based on her previous shopping experiences."

Jennifer smiled as she remembered. "She said to me, 'Jen, I just realized I've never been asked *may I help you* in any of your three shops.

I always feel like I'm walking into a friend's home and being welcomed when I visit you.'

"I asked if she had told her friends about her experiences in my stores. She said she hadn't, but that she would make a point of doing so. And then she suggested a stationery party one afternoon with some wine, and she would invite six or seven of her friends.

"That was the beginning of creating my first 'raving fan,' and the stationery parties have been a tremendous marketing success. We've taken them into the homes and clubs of our customers, increased our market share—we have so many more customers now—and have opened two more shops. We continually listen to our customers. We make a point to build relationships with them and encourage their input."

Gregg exchanged glances with Mac, impressed.

Mac gestured to Jennifer. "Tell Gregg about how you opened your second and third stores," he prompted.

Jennifer leaned forward eagerly. "Pretty early on, when we still just had one store, our accountant and his brother had a falling out and his brother bought the practice. I liked Daniel and felt he enjoyed retailing, so I asked him if he was interested in joining our company. After he discussed the option with his wife, he said he would like to take care of our accounting and financial needs, but it was still not a full-time position. So he suggested being shop manager as well.

"I said that Jordyn was the shop manager, but he cut me off. 'I am talking about opening a second shop!' he said. With that we began planning the opening of the second shop in a similar demographic area to this one, and it's beaten the numbers here by eighteen percent." She sat back, looking very proud of herself.

"How did you decide to open the third one?" Gregg asked.

"Well, it seemed to me two shops were not that difficult, so why not add another?" Jennifer laugh at her naiveté. "Daniel, Jordyn, and

I analyzed the opportunities and associated costs; on paper it was feasible. There was a new shopping plaza being constructed in an area with the same customer profile as our other two stores. Jordyn knew a young woman who was studying graphic art and had been a part-time associate while going to school. Jordyn felt she could manage the new shop with our help. Abbie Malcome was a real spark plug. She lit up the shop when she came in, and all of her customers adored her. She held down the part-time job, worked full time during the holidays, and made all A's in her studies. 'A true winner' was how Jordyn described her."

Jennifer paused for emphasis. "Gregg, I must tell you there is a gigantic difference between three shops and two. It was easy enough to physically open the shop, as we had the experience. But soon we realized our systems and procedures were not keeping up with our growth."

Turning to Mac, she asked, "Have you explained the life cycle of a business to Gregg?"

Mac nodded.

"Okay, then. Well, our business was in the growth stage, but our systems and procedures had matured. We kept trying to make them work. Daniel spent more time putting band-aids on them than running his shop, so his sales took a dip. Another profit leak!

"The managers and I were meeting one morning before we opened North Brooke, the third shop, for the day and we were all feeling pretty low. Not only were the systems and procedures outdated, there was tension between the three managers and between them and me. Our little happy family was facing a crisis and each of us had a different behavior pattern."

"The DiSC?" Gregg questioned.

Jennifer gave him a delighted smile. "Jordyn and I have both a high D and I behavior pattern, Daniel's is a D and C, and Abbie is the highest I you can imagine. When I am under pressure I become all D, and when Daniel is stressed his C rises to the top. Abbie seems to be the stabilizing one because she hates conflict and wants everyone to get along. So here we are in the middle of a heated discussion. I want to charge forward, Daniel wants to analyze every detail to death, and Abbie is trying to make jokes to lighten the atmosphere." She gave a brief laugh.

"I was feeling awful because I wanted to see the business grow and operate like it did when we had two shops. I was beating myself up because I agreed to add a third. I was conflicted between two thoughts: the business has been successful and hasn't been a burden versus why is everything falling apart?

"So I'm sulking, Daniel is in deep thought, and Abbie is reading some fashion magazine. The room was so quiet you could hear a pin drop."

Jennifer's expression unfocused slightly, as if she was lost in her recollection of that morning. "Suddenly I heard the coffee pot brewing and whiffed the vanilla aroma. No one had moved, so I was mystified. Abbie left to investigate and called us to come to the break room immediately. Four cups and a wonderful assortment of French pastries were sitting on the counter. That was the only time I can recall Abbie being at a loss for words. And next to the coffee maker was a little toy compass—one like you find in a Cracker Jack box."

"Daniel went to the back of the shop, Abbie to the sales area, and I returned to my office, all of us trying to determine who might be our mysterious host. As I entered the office I came face to face with who we now know as Mac. I am sure my 'Mac story' from here on is similar to the others you've heard."

Mac entered the conversation. "Like my other friends, some of whom you've already met, Jennifer had a good start on her business but needed some coaching as the business grew. I find most startup businesses either have a rocky start and are forced to close within the first few years, or they surmount that initial hurtle and begin a successful trend. Think about the life cycle, Gregg. A new business is definitely in the introduction stage. Once a company avoids the early pitfalls that trip up most new entities, the business can advance into the growth stage. Jennifer's shops were still in the growth stages when she and I met, but her systems and procedures had matured. More importantly, her management style had already passed the maturity stage and was trending downward on the decline side of the life cycle. I'll get back to that point later.

"Besides each of the key individuals having a different behavior styles and the rapid growth of the company, Jennifer did not have a direction or focus, nor was there a unity of purpose."

"Why do you say that?" asked Gregg.

Jennifer jumped back in. "When Mac and I started talking and he asked me where I saw my business ten or twenty years from now, I couldn't answer him. How can anyone think that far into the future when they are up to their necks with crises and putting out fires? When we discussed the current operation, I realized each of the three shops was being managed differently. And I was having difficulty in going to the markets and trade shows while trying to keep an eye on all three shops. I was terrible at delegation and tried to micromanage Jordyn, Daniel, and Abbie. We all wanted the businesses to be successful, yet we were stuck and couldn't figure out how to get to the next level."

Having been mentally comparing Jennifer's issues to those of his own business, Gregg was truly beginning to understand Mac's logic. Mac was not telling him what to do; rather he was helping Gregg self-discover his own issues and their possible solutions. Now he understood why Mac had encouraged him to be the "owner" of both the issues and solutions. Hell, he was tired of all of his headaches and trying to cure them with the same passé medicine. There was a place for aspirin, but not in his business. Never again would he settle for short-term pain relief!

"I want to show you something." Jennifer rose walked to her desk, opened her top drawer, and pulled out the compass Mac had given her.

"The light is dawning!" Gregg exclaimed. "The compass is your reminder to plot a direction and stay the course."

Jennifer smiled. "You are a quick learner."

Gregg laughed. "If only you knew!"

Jennifer raised her eyebrows a little as if she understood that it had taken him some time to get to the point of accepting Mac's wisdom and methods. But as she sat down again she continued as if she had no idea. "To plot the direction and stay the course, as you say, you must first start with knowing where the beginning point is. Before I could figure out where I wanted to be in ten to twenty years I had to know where I was today. In other words, what is my business, how do I define it? I had to know first what game I was playing." She winked at Mac as she mimed tossing a football through the air in a perfect spiral. "At that time I carried only stationery and some invitations; I thought I was in the paper goods business. But with Mac's help, I now define my business as a supplier of upscale and unusual writing paraphernalia and services. With this new definition I went to my suppliers with a different mindset. I sought products and services to fill the needs of our customers in my particular segment of the market. I knew I could not be all things to all people, so I had to select a niche that matched my customers' needs.

"We conducted a variety of focus groups to solicit customer input. We shopped the competition to understand how to differentiate ourselves from them, and then we formed an advisory group made up of our banker, lawyer, CPA, and a business coach we hired to be a sounding board for our strategy and to make sure we had the available resources necessary to fund and support our growth and direction.

"It was an eye opener to see as the process unfolded—and how we'd come as far as we did without a business plan or a budget! I had everything in my head and Daniel seemed be taking care of the money okay. At least, I didn't receive any calls about not paying bills or the bank saying we were overdrawn.

"I remember Will Allen, our business coach, came by for our regular get-together and I asked if his other clients were ever in the same situation I was in. He responded that many were or had been, but it didn't make me feel any better. At that time Will and I had only been working together for a few months. I kept referring to him as a consultant and he kept correcting me by saying he was my coach, mentor, and partner. It took me a while to understand the difference, but the longer we worked together, the more I realized how he was helping me self-discover my issues, as Mac spoke about earlier. Will had been in retailing and had coached a wide variety of other kinds of businesses and organizations. I would fuss at him good naturedly because he would not simply give me the answers I wanted. My D was in high gear and I wanted to know the bottom line. He would say no one knows my business better than I do, and with Mac's preparatory training I was ready to discover our next level."

Jennifer reached out a finger and spun the compass around on the table. "On one of Will's first visits to my office he noticed the compass on my desk and asked me about it. I told him it was my reminder to plot a business course and stay focused. He wholeheartedly agreed. The two of us outlined my goals both from a business and a personal point of view and prioritized them. We talked about the present business and reviewed the findings of our focus groups and our competitive posture. I told him I was comfortable that when we needed capital for growth, the banks would be there; but they wanted a business plan and the accompanying financials. So we worked on the documents with Daniel, and in a relatively short time we presented them to the advisory committee. They tweaked them here and there and added some great input. Now we know who we are and how we define our business; we have our map and dashboard."

"Map and dashboard?" Gregg asked.

Jennifer smiled. "That's what Will called them. He gave me this example. Over the years he discovered that the majority of his clients spent more time planning a vacation than they did planning their business."

Gregg gave Mac the briefest of glances, enough to see the small smile on the carpenter's face.

"I told him that was absurd," Jennifer continued, "but he convinced me to look at the example first before I criticized it. I remembered Mac's comment about listening to understand before speaking to be understood. So I tried. Will asked me these two simple questions to help my self-discovering:

"Would I take a cross country trip without a road map?

"Would I cover my car's dashboard during the trip?

"It took me only a minute or two to see where he was going with these inquiries. The road map is the business plan and the dashboard is all the business indicators I need to monitor my business—like my budget, my financials, my competitive advantage, my traffic counts of customers, and so forth." She leaned towards Gregg. "Gregg, the key word is *my* because I am the owner of these."

Gregg held up his hand. "Let me get this straight. I'll use myself as an example. We—my wife Elaine and I—took a trip to Seattle a few years ago. I remember having a series of maps for the trip. I also prebooked reservations across the country for places we wanted to stay. We planned side trips and allocated extra time in some places in order to see the sights and not be rushed. I used the Internet and Web sites to help. I bet I spent several weeks planning that trip. We were able to see everything we wanted and never felt stressed out." He shook his head, looking at Mac. "I sure have been spending more time planning personal events than planning my business. When you look at it that way, it seems crazy!"

Mac smiled encouragingly. "So what about the dashboard; how does that fit in?"

Gregg thought for a moment. "On my trip I watched all the gauges. Sometimes we were miles from a service station and I had to make sure I had plenty of gas. I also always check the oil and temperature when I'm traveling. I guess that gas equates to the cash position in the business. The oil is another business resource—maybe like our inventory—and the temperature could be our accounts receivables and payables. How's that, Mac? Am I getting it now?" he asked with genuine delight.

"Gregg, you are a good student at picking up these ideas," Mac said. Then he cautioned, "I'll pay you another visit in the future to see how well you're using this new knowledge. Remember, it's not just what you are *learning*; it's much more important to own and use the information to change lives, beginning with yours."

Jennifer added, "I would constantly find myself gravitating back to my old ways. I truly had to make a conscious effort to change my outlook and use the gifts that Mac brought me. I tell you, these are gifts—and I have shared them with the others to create our unity of purpose."

"You'd better explain 'unity of purpose.' It sounds as if I'll need to add this to my notebook," responded Gregg.

Mac laughed, rising from his seat. "You're learning, Gregg. Even if you don't know the answers, you can always ask someone who does. Why don't I get us some more coffee and Jennifer can keep giving you the details."

He refilled the coffee cups while Gregg snagged a piece of French pastry; Jennifer, however, was clearly so engrossed in her explanation that she didn't touch her steaming hot cup.

"Let's discuss two concepts: first we had to implement a direction and focus for Ashley's Fine Stationery, and second we had to understand the different behavior styles we each have within the company. Remember Mac's triangle where there was little planning and communications but plenty of fires? We had to greatly improve our planning process and effectively communicate our plans among all of the associates within the company. We were committed to doing things right the first time and moving out of our crisis environment."

"Jordyn, Daniel, Abbie, and I took a long weekend to begin developing our first ever business plan. It was hard for me in the beginning. I was stressing over what was occurring at the shops, and I kept checking my cell phone for messages, even though the other three left strict orders for us not to be disturbed except for an extreme emergency.

"I gave my notes from Mac to Daniel to be our facilitator. He was the most detailed one of us and good at not rushing through our deliberation. To keep Abbie from becoming bored, she was appointed to keep all the notes. I told her we were all depending on her to keep accurate minutes. In truth, it was to keep her mind focused on the details, which is rather hard for a High I behavior style. So we made a list of all our issues, put them in similar groups, and then prioritized the groups. Then we began our action planning process."

Gregg raised his hand as if a student in school, but Jennifer cut him off.

"I know, Gregg; you want to know the meaning of the action planning process. It's a series of action plans that takes us beyond talking a good game into implementing the actions we must take. By putting a plan down on paper, we ensure that our direction or road map is clearly understood, and we increase our opportunity to achieve a higher level of success."

Jennifer moved to the bookcase behind her desk and took down a three ring binder. She sat down next to Gregg and opened the binder on the table in front of them. "Here's a hard copy of the PowerPoint presentation we used during our planning sessions.

"As you can see, on this page we start out with this sheet entitled 'The Process,' which is exactly what it says. It's a process to take us to our next level. It's simple in concept, but the challenge most of us face is actually implementing The Process and taking the time to plan and communicate. But I assure you it is worth the effort.

"Our busiest times of the year are the major holidays. Christmas is the most active, as we have many unique gifts our customers enjoy giving. As a result of being tremendously involved in the numerous activities that take place in that fourth quarter of the year, we devote very little time to planning for the following year. When we finally got around to talking about the next year, it was already late January or early February, which meant it was time to go to the markets and trade shows to pick out our spring merchandise.

"When we would sit down as a group, we usually only discussed a few goals, some ideas as to how we might achieve them, and occasionally we might create an actual objective. Typically if and when we began to make progress, the phone would ring and interrupt our meeting with the latest crisis. One of us would have to put on our fire equipment and go out to deal with fires. By the time we returned to this so-called planning we had lost our interest, and our intensity was on the new crisis. We had lost any drive we might have had for planning the future."

Gregg winced. Jennifer was describing his own planning process. "I believe that Mac's rubbed off on you. You seem to be reading my mind as well as he does. Am I that transparent?"

Jennifer laughed. "It's not that, Gregg. Most businesses have the same issues. I've shared this same information with many others and their reactions are practically the same. Most people say it seems so easy;

if only they had known about these concepts years ago. As a hobby I check to see how other companies I interact with have performed using this information. The ones that embrace it have seen great improvement. The remainder is still taking two aspirins and trying to cure their relentless headaches instead of addressing their issues or symptoms."

Pointing to the open page, she continued, "This is a diagram of my explanation. Look at this part. When we first started talking about objectives I was the only 'owner.' It didn't take me long to realize I needed to delegate to Jordyn, Daniel, and Abbie. I knew they were all interested in the success of our business, but I couldn't expect their involvement to be the same as mine. It was *my* business. I was the one whose signature was on the loans. I was the one waking up at three a.m. either in a panic or ready to jump out of bed to implement my latest brainstorm. Mac helped me to understand that my employees' motivation and involvement were different than mine, so I needed to have them relate the business to something personal for them."

Gregg stopped his note taking and said, "It reminds me of the hen and the pig. When you eat bacon and eggs for breakfast you have to remember the hen was only involved, while the pig was totally committed."

Mac laughed out loud, but Jennifer took Gregg's unique humor a little more seriously. "You have a point. We all want to be involved in our success, but I have a bigger stake in the involvement. I often feel my neck is on the line."

Continuing, she explained, "I asked each of the three managers to share with me some of the personal goals they wanted to accomplish. I asked them to give some real thought before they answered. After we met and each had discussed their aspirations, we linked them to our business. In other words, we tied in their personal goals to our business goals and then related them to the objectives of the company. I wanted their 'want to's' whether they were personal or business goals. This part of The Process helped to create our unity of purpose. Now we're all beginning to move in the same direction."

"To make the delegation process effective I broke down each objective into four phases." Jennifer turned the page in her binder for Gregg to see. "I created a simple word for each: What, How, Who, and When. Once you understand the meaning of each, the big picture of The Process becomes clearer."

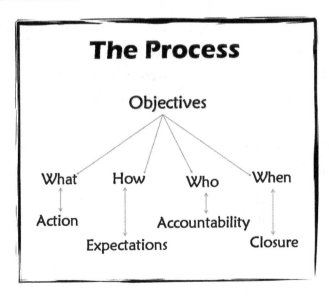

"Most business owners and managers have the What, which they refer to as their to-do list. But I've noticed most of the business owners I know never complete their to-do lists, and the bottom half is either postponed or forgotten altogether. In The Process, the What describes actions needed to accomplish a specific goal, function, or task.

"The How is most important. It explains the expectations of each action to be taken. We spend as much time as needed on identifying the How because it helps eliminate most of the assumptions between those performing and those requesting the actions to take place. For example, one day I told Jordyn to figure out what she could do to increase sales. The next week I noticed on our flash report that her sales were up but the margins were down. The next time I was in her shop I asked her how she'd accomplished this. She gave a boastful answer: 'I put a few items on sale and called our best customers to notify them.' What could I say? I hadn't given her enough information; I just assumed she would do something else. I was at fault, not Jordyn." She spread her hands helplessly, then ticked off two fingers.

"To me, the two most troublesome pronouns in business are *we* and *they*. Gregg, think about it this way. You give an action to a group and tell 'them' to do it. If it isn't accomplished, and it usually isn't, whom do you talk to? There is no accountability with these pronouns. Therefore, the Who establishes accountability both for the actions and the supporting expectations. During a meeting with Jordyn, Daniel, and Abbie, I mentioned it would be good to come up with an interesting window display for Mother's Day. I assumed at least one of the three would pick up the ball and run with it. Wrong! Not only was no one accountable, in their minds they each had more than they could handle.

"So many times we end a conversation with a conversation. That is, we talk and talk but don't achieve the closure we need. The When gives us closure by setting time frames or specific times as well as follow-up dates to accomplish a given action."

Jennifer shifted her binder around and turned to the tab marked 'Sales and Marketing.' Showing it to Gregg, she explained, "Here is the Action Plan section for our sales and marketing initiatives. Included are two action plans I want to review with you. The first is to increase sales in each shop by a minimum of fifteen percent for the third fiscal quarter. The second action plan is to create, design, and implement a window display for each shop for Father's Day."

Gregg turned the binder towards him and followed the two examples as Jennifer explained each.

ACTION PLAN-- Increase sales in each shop by a minimum of 15% for the first fiscal quarter.				
WHAT	**HOW**	**WHO**	**WHEN**	**STATUS**
Determine what categories and items should be promoted for the January Sale scheduled the weekend of the 18th	➢ Review the inventory reports to identify excess merchandise	**Daniel** Shop Managers	December 15th	
	➢ Contact vendors to determine if they have after Christmas inventory specials	Jennifer	December 15th	
Identify available advertising dollars	➢ Review the advertising budget and vendor co-op funds for available promotional dollars	**Jordyn** Jennifer	December 15th	
	➢ Based on available promotional dollars contact the newspapers to secure advertising space	Daniel	December 27th	
Determine how to increase the Valentine's Day Promotion	➢ Evaluate the last three Valentine's Day promotions	**Abby** Jordyn Daniel	January 7th	
	➢ Evaluate the possibility and costs of adding a newspaper insert	Daniel	January 7th	
	➢ Determine the labor costs and coverage needed		January 7th	
	➢ Project sales, costs, and margins associated with this promotion	**Daniel** Shop Managers		

ACTION PLAN-- Increase sales in each shop by a minimum of 15% for the first fiscal quarter.				
WHAT	**HOW**	**WHO**	**WHEN**	**STATUS**
	➤ Make a decision	Daniel	January 7th	
Create a "Raving Fans" referral program for each weekend in March	➤ Discuss with customers visiting the shops if they would like to host a stationary party. (Goal is four parties per shop)	**Jennifer** Shop Managers **Jordyn** Shop Managers	January 10th On or before February 14th	
	➤ Telephone preferred customer list if additional names are required			
	➤ Hold initial meeting with identified hosts	**Jordyn** Shop Managers	February 16th	
Develop a budget for each event and project a revised first quarter budget	➤ Analyze projected sales, margins and costs to estimate the likely financial outcome for each event and the quarter	**Jordyn** Shop Managers	February 23	
	➤ Finalize the events for the first quarter	**Daniel** Jennifer Shop Managers	December 15th	
		Jennifer Shop Managers	December 15th	

Gregg was impressed with the detail—and yet the action plan was clear and not complicated. He leaned closer as Jennifer showed the next one.

ACTION PLAN-- Create, design and implement a window display for each shop for Father's Day				
WHAT	**HOW**	**WHO**	**WHEN**	**STATUS**
Determine what items will be displayed and which items to be featured	➤ Select items that would be unique gifts for any man	**Jennifer** Store Managers	May 1st	
	➤ Choose the featured items in our three price categories	**Jennifer** Store Managers	May 1st	
Develop a concept for the display and plan-a-gram	➤ Create a theme that goes beyond the father to include other male relatives, mentors, etc.	**Jennifer** Store Managers	May 1st	
Order inventory based on needs	➤ Based on the above place inventory orders within budgeting guidelines	Daniel	May 5th	
Order displays	➤ Order display material and signs	Abbie	May 5th	
Evaluate the window display	➤ Make a physical site inspection of each window display	**Abbie** Shop Managers	June 15th	
Track the sales of featured items	➤ Determine success of featured items and overall success of the event	**Daniel** Jennifer Shop Managers	June 20th	

Then Jennifer directed his attention back to the first action plan. "The overall plan itself is identified in the heading, and there are five columns to break the plan down. Column one is the What, or actions required to achieve the plan. These are well thought out to ensure we are taking the correct actions to achieve the plan or accomplish the objective. The second column is the How, or expectations. You can see there is more than one expectation for most of the actions. The third column establishes accountability with the Who. Notice that the name in bold letters is the accountable person. Only one person can be accountable, although he or she may have others helping accomplish the tasks. Then, there is a When, or a date to accomplish the action—as I said earlier, to achieve closure on a particular action. If a specific date or timeframe cannot be determined then follow-up dates are used.

"I told you prior to this action plan that the window display for Mother's Day was a complete disaster and it was my fault. I assumed if I threw out the bait, one of the shop managers would bite, take the idea, and create a display. I was setting everyone up for failure, including me. Now, I have incorporated the lessons from Mac and remembered to use the compass he gave me. I plan better, I communicate more effectively, and most of all I have more time for myself." She cocked her head thoughtfully. "Gregg, you might say I reestablished my own sanity.

"As we practiced using the action planning technique we improved our planning skills." Pointing to the second action plan, she continued, "This plan goes beyond creating a window display. It includes inventory needs, designing of the window, creating display material that will add the 'other men in your life besides Dad,' evaluating the display at each shop, and creating a method for tracking the sales to be better prepared for the next Father's Day."

By the time Jennifer finished her explanations and closed the binder, Gregg was worried. "I don't know how in the world I'm going to find the time to go into that much depth. Moreover, you have three shops in three different locations. All my business is under one roof!"

Mac held up a hand. "And how productive has your time been, or that of your staff? Remember our comparisons of your daughter's party and the sales meeting? You could give a full accounting of the details you planned for your vacation. You will spend far less time using the action planning process than putting out the fires you create. You won't be spending so much time in the office, especially on the weekends. Who knows, you may have time to improve your golf game and tennis serve."

Gregg didn't respond, but he knew both Jennifer and Mac were accurate with their comments. *But where do I begin?* he wondered. *How do I incorporate these techniques into my business? Can my staff learn to use them, or more importantly, do I have the ability to teach them?*

Jennifer broke into his thoughts. "I will caution you again, Gregg. It's much easier to watch someone else go through the planning and communicating process we've discussed this morning. When I went on my trip with Mac, I said to myself I couldn't wait to get back to work and put into practice all that I experienced. The first couple of weeks I put my shoulder to the wheel, but after that I almost allowed my old ways to take over. Remember, it may seem like this process is difficult and takes a long time. That's because you're doing the work up-front, which you've never done before. Once you start to realize that you don't have to do so much work on the back end and at the last minute, you'll begin to appreciate the time you spend planning."

She favored Mac with a smile of gratitude. "I am so appreciative to Mac for prodding me forward to be innovative with new ideas and most of all to change the environment of the company. I find I have much more time available to devote to accomplishing both my personal and business goals. My stress barometer is registering calm. For me, starting the process began by starting with me. I had to change."

And that was that. As she walked them to the door, Jennifer said to Gregg, "Think of me as your sister in business. Listen to Mac. I'm living proof his ideas and concepts are valid. If I can ever help you with anything, please give me a call."

Mac and Gregg said their thanks and headed to the red pickup. Once inside Gregg shouted "I am so excited! I know I'm only seeing the very basics and that it will take a great deal of practice to get it right. But I am resolving here and now in this 1946 Ford pickup"—he patted the dashboard—"that I will commit to these concepts and be an owner of my issues and solutions."

Mac replied, "You're a great student, especially when you want to be. I have full confidence that you'll do what is necessary to change your life and the lives of others. Now, reach into the glove compartment."

Gregg was prepared to tap the screen, but to his amazement there was only a small gold star. "What's this?"

"It's your gold star. You've earned it, and as long as you continue in this manner you can keep it." Mac smiled. "And don't worry, I'll be checking to make sure you deserve to wear it."

"Thanks, Mac." Gregg stuck it onto his shirt. "Where are we off to next? Another mysterious rendezvous?"

Mac smiled and responded, "No, not really. We are finally going to get to the heart of the matter."

Gregg gave a mock order: "Drive on, Mac. I can't wait to see what's in store for me and our next adventure." Taking out his notepad once again, he wrote:

notes

✓ Plot a direction and stay the course. Remember the compass!

✓ Use your business plan and budget as the map and dashboard of your business.

✓ Listen to the customer. The customer votes for goods or services they want with the dollars they spend.

✓ Learn how to create and maintain "raving fans."

✓ Build lasting relationships with customers- the best advertising is a satisfied customer.

notes

✓ Preconditioning creates our shopping experiences. Make sure you provide an experience for your customers that differentiates you from the masses.

✓ Know your business and be able to define and focus it by using customer votes.

✓ Make sure your employees have a "unity of purpose"-define we and they.

✓ Self-discover your own issues and solutions; be the owner of both.

✓ Form a group of your key advisors.

✓ Develop an action planning process using What, When, Who, and How.

✓ Stick with changes until they become part of the business culture.

✓ Only one individual can be accountable... eliminate 'we' and 'they'.

Chapter 8

At their next destination, Gregg stepped out onto the pavement in front of Benson's Medical Supplies. The thing he noticed was that the sun was in the exact same position when he walked out of his house.

Benson's Medical Supplies was not a tall building but it took up over an acre of land. Delivery trucks were being maneuvered into loading bays and he could see the movement of forklifts inside a warehouse.

"This is the first time we haven't entered through a front door," Gregg said as they walked to the rear stairs.

"I know," replied Mac, "But this is where we'll find David."

Even this early in the morning, a flurry of activity was taking place, and each employee appeared to know exactly what he was doing. Mechanized conveyor systems were in full operation; the whole system clearly functioned like a well-oiled machine.

Mac walked into the employees' lounge and bought two cups of coffee from the vending machine. "Not exactly a china cup," Gregg noticed. "Mac, can I treat you to a Twinkie? I doubt if there are any French pastries hanging around."

Mac took the cup as they sat down in the molded fiberglass chairs. *It may not be the fanciest lunchroom I have been in, but it is one of the cleanest*, thought Gregg as he sipped. Then the door opened and a tall, handsome man in his forties entered, laughing and waving behind him at another employee. From their body language and facial expressions, Gregg guessed the two had known each other a long time and must be talking about something non-work-related. The second man continued on down the hall; when the first man looked in their direction his face lit up, and he sat down at the table with Mac and Gregg, straddling a chair. There was complete silence at the table, and Gregg felt a little uncomfortable. Both Mac's and this stranger's eyes were closed and their heads slightly bowed.

"Amen," escaped from the man's lips, and the two shook hands. Looking towards Gregg he added, "I always say a prayer of thanks when Mac arrives safe and sound from one of his trips."

Mac introduced them. "David, say hello to Gregg Herbert. Gregg, this is David Banks. David is the third generation to head up this business, and he's doing an excellent job."

"Hi, Gregg, glad to meet you." David reached across the table to shake hands. "The 'excellent job' is as much because of Mac as anything I may be doing. But a compliment from him is always welcomed."

Gregg turned to look at Mac. "Do your friends always know when you're coming to visit?"

"I'll answer that," responded David. "And the answer is an emphatic yes and no. We never know when Mac and one of his visitors will arrive, but they always come at the right time and we enjoy sharing our experiences.. Being with Mac never lasts long enough."

David got up and put quarters in the vending machine. "I was walking around the warehouse with one of our new forklift drivers," David explained. "He's on his orientation, and I always like to meet our new associates and thank them for joining our company."

So much for my theory of old friendships, Gregg thought. He pulled out his notebook and with the ever-sharp, stubby yellow pencil made a note to himself to meet all of his new employees personally and get to know them. He realized that in all of his orientation meetings, he merely gave a general "pep talk," as he had intended to do at the one scheduled later in his morning. Now he could see that wasn't enough. He placed a star next to improving HR and at the same time checked to see if his gold star was still on his collar. It was, and he was going to keep it.

As David joined them again with his hot chocolate, Gregg also noticed a star like his on David's shirt pocket. Gregg was feeling a little jittery at this point, and he wished he had hot chocolate as well instead of coffee.

David continued, "Gregg, I've met many of Mac's new friends so I know your visit with me comes towards the end of your outing. He brings 'clients' here as sort of a recap of what they have been exposed to. If you haven't noticed, Mac is a wonderful teacher and coach—he just has a strange sense of humor. Did he say you were going to 'the heart of the matter'?"

Gregg nodded.

"He used his humor to come up with that phrase; a great deal of our products are for cardiovascular patients," David explained, and with that they all had a good laugh.

Then David stood up, encouraging his visitors to follow. "Let's go to my office and I will set up the PowerPoint presentation Mac likes for me to review."

Walking from the warehouse to the administration offices, they passed both warehouse and office personnel. David knew not only their names but also something interesting about each. Arriving at his administrative assistant's desk, he briefly checked for messages.

"I've handled all but one of your telephone messages as well as all of your e-mail," reported the secretary, whose desk name placard read Tina Croswell. "You have a meeting in an hour with Robert."

Gregg could hardly believe his ears. He made a mental note to speak to his own secretary about how this kind of system might be possible. Nancy had been complaining for months for him to give her more to do, as she was looking for any kind of work to occupy her time. He winced slightly as he thought of her exact words: "to make the day move faster so I can get out of here."

Inside his office, David opened his laptop and pulled up the Pow-erPoint program. When he was ready all eyes went to the screen.

"Gregg, you may have seen bits and pieces of this presentation during your visit, but let's take a quick review."

Slide one was the Life Cycle diagram showing the various stages where systems, procedures, plans, and any other issues could occur si-multaneously within all aspects of the business. David summarized, "Knowing where each stage of business is positioned on the life cycle is key."

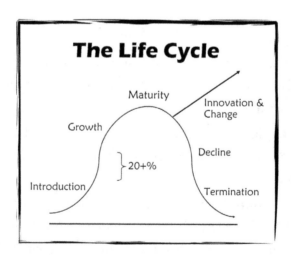

Slide two emphasized the need for better planning and effective com-munications. David reminded Gregg that it was vital to convert a busi-ness from being reactive to becoming proactive. "It takes too long and too much energy to keep putting out the fires."

Slide three dealt with everyone being on the same page, rather than assuming employees understood what management expected of them. "Requests for results or information may appear clear to one person without being understood by another," David said, emphasizing, "It's essential to take out the guesswork."

Gregg nodded his agreement and understanding.

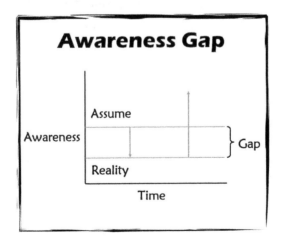

"Slide four illustrates how 'the road to hell is paved with good intentions,'" David continued with a laugh. "We cannot only go though the motions of planning and creating objectives, we must actually accomplish them. I am sure you have heard the expression that you not only have to talk the talk you *must* walk the walk! And if you need the support of your associates in accomplishing your goals you have to have their 'want to's.' Tying in their personal goals to your business goals aids in solidifying the process."

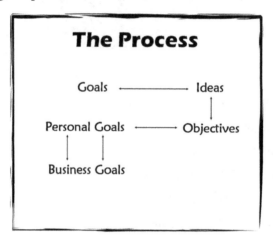

David clicked the screen again. "Slide five emphasizes the need for creating actions to support the objective while establishing the expectations of each. Accountability and closure are the two remaining elements of the action planning process. Only one person can be accountable for each action, and closure helps in reducing procrastination by establishing dates and timelines."

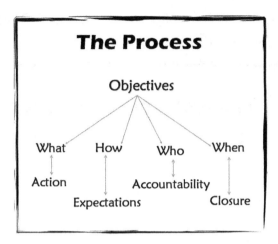

"This slide represents how all the previous ones come together," David summarized. "Let's start with the overall plan. Some people call it a strategic plan, a five-year plan or a business plan. The title is less important than its content. It must contain the following."

Gregg opened his notebook again and wrote as David listed:

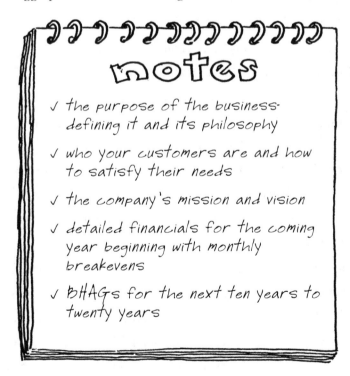

notes

✓ the purpose of the business- defining it and its philosophy

✓ who your customers are and how to satisfy their needs

✓ the company's mission and vision

✓ detailed financials for the coming year beginning with monthly breakevens

✓ BHAGs for the next ten years to twenty years

"This is what Mac calls 'the heart of the matter,'" David explained, switching to the final slide.

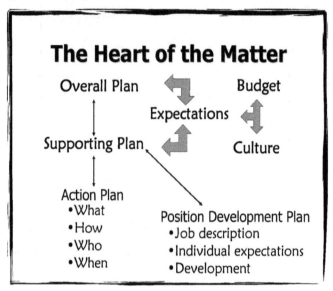

Gregg figured he was gathering enough information to at least begin a plan—except… "David, what is a BHAG?"

"A Big, Hairy, Audacious Goal," David said with a glint in his eyes, "but let me come back to that question.

"The supporting plan or plans are how the individual departments support the overall plan. For example, we need to know the status of Research and Development to blend them into our growth objectives. Or, what additional resources does Manufacturing need to meet promised delivery date? Or how does Logistics accomplish one of our mission statements for having the right product at the right price at the right time?"

He tapped the computer. "As you can see on the screen, the word that ties the two plans together is *expectations*. That was an important ingredient lacking in my organization until Mac showed up. Expectation at Benson's is a major part of our philosophy. Gregg, we want everyone, and I mean everyone, to understand what is expected on them; that is, they not only perform the duties of their position to the best of their ability, they must achieve the company's objectives as well. This concept applies from entry-level positions up to and including me. When this philosophy became part of our culture, our business took off to our next level. Now we are laying the foundation for our BHAGs.

"As you can see, *expectations* is the center word on this diagram. It links our entire business and ties in our strategic and tactical initiatives to our culture and to our budget. The culture is the way we want to 'live at work'; it is our philosophy of how we treat all of our associates, our vendors, and most of all our customers. I hear all too often that the purpose of a business is to make a profit. We don't look at profit as a purpose; we look at profit as a yardstick. Our purpose is to create and grow our customer base. How well we grow it is measured in profitability.

"The budget is another of our yardsticks. If the overall plan is our map, then the budget is our dashboard." He nodded as Gregg perked up at the familiar terms. "If our budget had a dashboard, it would tell us our cash position and what kind of return we were earning on our resources; and it is my best indicator of the return I am receiving on my time investment. My goal is to decrease my involvement in the daily operations while increasing sales, profits and efficiencies. When I can accomplish this goal then I am increasing the return on my time. Now I have the luxury of time to devote to creating a vision and to accomplishing our BHAGs."

"Okay, David, it's time to tell me more about the BHAGs," Gregg reminded him.

David grinned. "BHAGs, as I said earlier, are Big, Hairy, Audacious Goals. I meet with my executive staff off-site annually to discuss where we want to be in ten to twenty years. This is a radical departure from our strategic planning and budgeting process. We don't look at current activities; instead, we get out of the box and put no limit on our dreams."

Listening intently to David, Gregg mused, *I hope I'm using all three of the ears Mac mentioned.* "Can you give me an example of getting out of the box and the 'no limit' idea?"

"Sure," David said easily, sipping his hot chocolate. "In a typical planning session we might discuss increasing sales or revenues a certain percent. Or we could discuss adding to our facilities or developing new products. These thoughts are based on previous history, trends, the economy, market dynamics, and so forth. When we talk about a BHAG, it might be that we want to become the largest medical supplier in the world. Another could be that we want to be the number one resource to develop, produce, and patent the most innovative new products in the medical field. If it sounds like we're a bit crazy then we're usually on track to identify a BHAG."

"Then what do you do?" asked Gregg excitedly. BHAGs sounded like a lot more fun than their name implied.

"We pick the BHAGs we feel have the most merit and focus all our efforts on the short-term goals, building our way to reaching these stretch goals. Gregg, my personal timeframe for long-term planning is what we do for the next eighteen to twenty-four months, not the next five years. So, you must be thinking why in the world am I interested in a BHAG that is ten to twenty years in the future.

"See if this example helps. You love to travel and want to take a trip around the world. Let that be your BHAG. You are going to travel eastward, so your first destination is probably Europe or Africa. Consider that to be an intermediate goal. Traveling from here to that first continent is going to take most of your time and attention; therefore, consider that to be the first year's goal, something short-term. But you aren't planning to return home after the first leg of your around-the-world trek, so the first leg is also the beginning of reaching your BHAG.

"One final word—if you don't enjoy the preparation for the trip and each leg of the journey, then reaching the end of your destination will have little or no meaning. You have to learn to have fun in the planning process so you will enjoy managing your business. As Mac will tell you, business should be fun; and it all starts with planning and communications, the most basic of basics in any business."

Gregg could begin to see some logic to David's explanation, but he knew he would have to mull this over for a while and let the words sink in.

"Now, at the bottom of the diagram, you see the action plans and the position development plans, or PDPs as we refer to them." Looking at his watch David said, "If you have another hour I am meeting with Robert Forrest, our VP of Human Resources, in just a few minutes. We are going over some PDPs for our second tier level of management, and three of these managers report to me."

Gregg glanced over for Mac's okay. "Do we have the time to stay?"

"Of course, I wouldn't want you to miss this part," Mac answered.

They chatted for a few minutes about Gregg's previous visits, and Gregg admitted to his recent transformation from reluctant observer to enthusiastic student. Precisely on the hour they heard a knock on David's open door. Robert Forrest entered the office and David made the introductions.

"Robert, I want to have this conversation as if there were no visitors in our presence," he instructed.

Robert nodded. "You have three direct reports whose salary reviews are due in two weeks," he started. "I need to begin preparing the paperwork for their performance reviews and determine whatever increase you have in mind to fit into our budgeting criteria."

Gregg was writing furiously in his notebook. As he listened to the conversation unfold, he realized he was never timely with a salary review. Hell, no one in his company got one on time, including himself. Sometimes they were overlooked for months. He recalled that last month a longtime employee had left the company because he hadn't received a raise in two years. Thinking about it, Gregg realized in all the crisis management and putting out fires of the business the man had been overlooked. *He was a good employee, and that should have never happened*, he thought, remembering that he'd only found out about the man's resignation last week and quite by accident. Connecting pay increases to a budget had never once entered his mind. If they had money they gave out raises, and if there was no cash available it was just tough.

He came back to David and Robert's conversation. David was asking, "How did the three perform against their PDPs?"

Opening the first of three folders on his desk, Robert replied, "Billy maxed out. He accomplished all of his assigned goals as well as his development plans for the last six months. If fact, he enrolled at Salisbury College a semester ahead of his schedule to begin work on his MBA."

Thumbing through the second file he continued, "Jonathan did okay, but not as well as he should have. He still has a communication issue with his supervisors. I see in the file he reviewed with his team their DiSC profiles as well as his own, but when it came to using the action plans he tried to beat the system. I had to discuss this with him a few times to make sure that the Hows were clear and the Whens didn't slip in several of his action plans. But he's making improvements and I'll follow up with him according to his PDP. We have specific time slots scheduled.

"Grady is the problem child," Robert said, turning to the third file. "He's had many opportunities to address his weaknesses, and I've made sure we are communicating and had him repeat to me and write a recap of what he should be working on and how he would accomplish his PDP goals. We drafted a development plan for him, but he hasn't made one effort to improve. It is hard for me to grasp his 'want to's' even after all the counseling time we have spent. What's so surprising is how long he's been with the company; no one knew how poor a performer he was until we embraced accountability as part of our expectations. He would say all the right things but then do whatever he wanted. He became lost in the shuffle of events. After these first six months working with Grady, though, I've confirmed my suspicions and will make sure he understands the peril he's brought upon himself.

"He hasn't bought into the action planning process and his mediocre results seem to prove that point. I've given him an oral review, but now it's time for a written one. Grady is well aware of our 'three strikes and you're out' policy, but he's still not an 'owner' of his consequences."

As Robert closed the folder, David said, "I want you to arrange for a written corrective review with Grady. If he won't take the ball I would like you to contact Myles at the outplacement service and make the preparations for his departure. He's now on thirty days probation. Please speak to Tina and find a time for the three of us to meet this afternoon."

Then David turned to Gregg and Mac, who were listening quietly to this rather somber turn of events. "Gregg, our employees are our most important asset, and we go out of our way to see they are successful. On very rare occasions termination is required, and we understand the havoc that can occur. But I have a company to run; I cannot put it or the other employees in jeopardy because of a few bad apples. I discovered a while back that if I ask three questions concerning a particular employee I usually have a good feel for what must be done."

Gregg picked up his pencil again. "And those are…?"

"The first one is whether I would hire that employee today knowing all I know now about him or her. The second question is if the employee came to me and said he or she were leaving, would I be upset or disappointed about that decision? The last one is whether this individual can ever be successful within the company. If there is a clear no answer to any of the three, then I have a real issue with that person. If the answers to two of the questions are no, then that calls for dramatic action on my part. I know turnover is one of the largest hidden costs a company bears, but allowing poor performance is not fair to either that employee or the company and its other employees. I will not award or encourage poor or mediocre performance."

Pulling his chair closer to Gregg's, he said, "I want to review a PDP with you. We'll use Billy's. This company had the basic job descriptions that most others use, but when we really examined them, we found they were inadequate. So we came up with Position Development Plans to help management and employees understand better what their jobs actually are."

Mac broke in. "Gregg, during my visits, I have seen job descriptions read once or twice by the employee and then stuck in a drawer or file never to be seen again. In many organizations, their only value is in establishing a description of the job and pay ranges."

David opened Billy's personnel file and took out the PDP.

Benson's Medical Supplies, Inc.
Associate Personal Development Plan

The Personal Development Plan will be used quarterly to assess and recognize the Associate's strengths, growth opportunities, career goals, and the Manager's role in supporting the development plan.

This information is considered privileged and should NOT be shared outside of the associate's direct chain of command or the human resources department.

(To be filled out by the Associate's Manager)

Associate Name: William H. Pearson
Position Title: Director of Logistics
Department: Operations
Reports to: David Banks, President
Direct Reports: Warehouse Manager, Transportation
Supervisor, Traffic Manager

Scope of Position:

The Director of Logistics is responsible for all functions of the warehouse and transportation to ensure the timely and accurate delivery of medical equipment and supplies to our customers. The Director will work closely with managers of sales, finance, and safety to fulfill the mission of the company and to adhere to all OSHA, state and local laws.

Primary Duties and Accountabilities:

- ✓ Directs activities, programs, and strategic plans throughout the warehouse and shipping while providing advice and knowledge to the other members of his/her team.

- ✓ Meets or exceeds agreed upon goals and objectives.

- ✓ Creates a positive environment for the entire warehouse and transportation team.

- ✓ Ensures all procedures and controls are in place for a safe and efficient culture.

- ✓ Develops direct reports by following company guidelines

- ✓ Always set the example for others in dress, attitude, and performance.

- ✓ Reports directly to the President

Associate Quarterly Review

Strength Review   *(To be completed by the associate)*

What were the three major accomplishments of the past quarter?
- ✓ Installed mechanized conveyor system

- ✓ Met all OSHA requirements and passed inspection

- ✓ Developed and promoted new traffic manager

Growth Opportunities   *(To be completed by the associate)*

What are my growth commitments to become more effective in my current position this quarter? (SMART GOAL – Specific, Measurable, Attainable, Relevant, Timely)

- ✓ Spend more time developing the Safety Manager
- ✓ Work with finance to understand associated costs
- ✓ Create a system for streamlining the handling of warranted products

Career Goals (Long Term)   *(To be completed by the associate)*

What are my long-term career goals?
- ✓ Receive a Masters of Logistic from State U
- ✓ Become a vice president of the company
- ✓ Retire by age 65

What are my long-term growth commitments for this quarter?
- ✓ Enroll at State U to begin my Masters' work
- ✓ Attend the industry's logistic seminar

Quarterly Personal Goals   *(To be completed by the associate)*

What are three personal goals to be completed within the next 3 months?

✓ Discuss with the VP of Human Resources my retirement plans

✓ Discuss with the President my career opportunities

✓ Spend more time with my sons

Manager Support

What support and/or resources do I need from my manager in order to accomplish my goals?   *(To be completed by the associate)*

✓ Discuss my career advancement with specified interim goals

What is my manager's commitment to support? *(To be completed by Manager)*

✓ Develop Billy and prepare him for becoming VP of Logistics

✓ Suggest other outside learning experiences

✓ Create a reading list for his career development

After an in-depth explanation of Billy's PDP, Gregg realized another hour had flown by when David announced, "Time to finish up here. I have another meeting in five minutes."

"Are most of your days filled with meetings?" Gregg inquired.

"Not really. I used to feel as if I was meeting to death," David said with a rueful laugh, "but Mac has coached me to develop a process to make our meetings productive—and they are. And one of the main principles is to start and end on time." Rising from his chair, he headed Mac and Gregg to Tina's desk. "Please feel free to spend as much time here as you would like. I'll have Tina make whatever arrangements you might need. If you have time I'll meet you for lunch.

Mac spoke. "Thanks, David, but we have one more stop before I take Gregg back home."

After the goodbyes, Mac and Gregg exited the way they entered and walked to the pickup. "So this is our next to last stop?" Gregg asked with disappointment in his voice.

Climbing into the truck, Mac replied, "Yes, one more and we will be through with this part of our journey. We'll be heading back towards your home. I don't want you to be late for work."

Gregg almost laughed, thinking of how worried he had been at the beginning of the day—and it was still the beginning! Pulling out his notebook he read:

notes

- ✓ Meet and get to know all new employees personally-they are the most important asset.

- ✓ Understand and use The Process.

- ✓ Remember the various points, events and processes on the Life Cycle.

- ✓ Reduce the fires in a crisis environment by planning and communication.

- ✓ Close the awareness gap.

- ✓ Get employees to "want to" and gain their support in The Process.

- ✓ Incorporate the What, How, Who and When into achieving objectives.

- ✓ Make a list of BHAGs-Big, Hairy, Audacious Goals.

notes

✓ Do not tolerate poor or mediocre performance.

✓ Start and stop meetings on time.

✓ Expectations tie the overall plan to the supporting plan as well as to the budget and culture.

✓ If you do not enjoy the preparations for a journey, you will not truly appreciate the destination.

✓ PDPs enable an employee to develop for the betterment of both the employee and the company.

✓ Salary and performance reviews must be meaningful, on time and tie into the PDPs.

✓ Turnover is one of the biggest "hidden expenses" in business, but allowing an employee to stay with the company who is not productive and has no "want to's" is more devastating.

Chapter 9

"Robert Camp inherited a hardware store three days after graduating from college," Mac told Gregg as he drove. "He's worked odd jobs during the summers at the store since the age of sixteen. The hardware store belonged to his uncle, who had no children, so he left the store to Robert with enough insurance to finance his first couple of years.

"Robert had a great work ethic and took the time to learn the details of the business. He selected two mentors, one with an extensive background in the tool industry, and a college professor he befriended.

"He spent long hours becoming acquainted with every aspect of the business. Robert didn't want to be 'another hardware store,' so he looked for ways to differentiate it from the masses. I'll let him tell you the rest of the story," Mac indicated as he parked the truck.

Ringing the rear entrance bell, he added, "Robert reminds me a lot of you, especially when you were his age starting your business life."

Gregg didn't miss the inference of Mac's remark but kept his thoughts to himself.

A young woman opened the door and asked how she could help them. Mac asked if Robert was in, giving only his first name. As she disappeared back through a maze of well-organized shelves, Gregg thought that this hardware store seemed rather unusual—many of the tools sported colored handles.

Then Robert appeared, a tall man who resembled a long distance runner. When he saw Mac he quickened his pace and gave Mac the type of greeting Gregg was coming to expect. Gregg was introduced and Robert led them towards the front of the store. Between the storage area and the display showroom, they passed a small classroom with a surrounding counter ledge that served as workspace. Various demonstrations were set up, including a lavatory, a sink, a door with frame, and broken pieces of furniture and glassware.

Gregg wondered what this workspace could possibly be used for. He also saw that there were more female than male associates straightening displays and replenishing goods, all wearing different colored aprons with their names and the company logo embroidered on the bib.

"We're starting a little earlier this morning," Robert explained. "Every Monday and Thursday at six thirty a.m. we have a class open to the public to learn how to do the most common small jobs and repairs around the house."

Robert continued, smiling at Gregg's expression. "I had only been managing the store for a short time when I realized I couldn't compete with the national chains on price. I had to figure out another way to attract business. When I spent time on the floor and talked to my customers, I realized the majority were single females heading up their households and responsible for all the bills. Many had children and as single mothers were juggling their time and dollars. They weren't able to have their repair questions answered to their satisfaction at the chain stores, so many would venture here looking for help without feeling intimidated.

"One day Diane Attaway entered the store looking for a hammer and a lavatory repair kit. She had a very petite frame and complained to the employee about the hammer being too large to fit her hand, and that the instructions on the kit were not clear. I introduced myself and within a few minutes learned she was a single mom with teenagers and watching her pennies. I talked her though the process of replacing the toilet valve system and acknowledged her comment about the hammer size. Then I told her to call me if she had any problems with the repair. Diane called later in the day to thank me for my help and for saving the cost of a plumber. She has been a 'raving fan' of ours ever since and has brought in many of her neighbors.

"One day while talking to my mentor, Phil Zahn, who was well experienced in the manufacturing of hand tools, I relayed the conversation I'd had with Diane. He took Diane's idea and created a new line of smaller hand tools for women. Phil even went a step further by holding focus groups and determining that women would like to have colored handles. His company followed their wishes—but with a twist. He color-coded the tools used for common repairs, and added instructions. If a Phillips-head screwdriver was needed, it was coded blue, and a blade screwdriver was green. This made the repair easier to understand for someone not familiar with tools.

"The women came in droves and a niche was created. So then we opened stores in the areas where the population included a large number of single female households, and now we have nine locations. And each has a classroom like we have here."

"What goes on in the classroom?" inquired Gregg.

"Come on back and see. The class is just beginning."

Following Robert to the classroom, they peered though the large glass window. The ten women had been divided into small groups moving from one demonstration area to another. They were learning how to repair a toilet, unclog a sink, replace a broken lock, and repair the seat of a chair. Each demo area was staffed with a female associate who patiently answered questions and gave each "student" a turn to make the required repair using the colored tools.

"These classes have set us apart from the competition and answer the repair needs of this population base," Robert said proudly.

While he left to meet a customer, Gregg asked Mac, "Why are we here? It seems Robert has all the answers. Why did he need a visit from you?"

Mac cryptically responded, "Robert has a High I behavior style. Watch him with his customer. See how he's using many hand gestures: he has a big smile and he keeps touching the customer on the shoulder. These are all indicators of a High I; most of all, I's like to talk and be helpful. It's very important to Robert that he be accepted and acknowledged by the customer. The same holds true in a group. In Robert's case the group was the original store; now he needs to feel acceptance from all nine of his stores.

"Robert hired college students close to his own age," Mac continued. "He didn't want to act like their boss; he wanted to be one of the gang. He was seldom in his office and met with the associates individually or in a group. At first this worked, but the business grew until these informal get-togethers were no longer productive. Robert kept trying to keep the same management style, but after the third store opened he became frustrated because his meetings were a disaster. Not one meeting was scheduled or had an agenda. Often the wrong people were involved, or required participants were out of town or otherwise busy, and necessary actions could not be addressed. Since Robert knew what was supposed to be discussed, he was the only one prepared for the discussions, and even that was limited."

Robert joined Mac and Gregg again, overhearing the last part of Mac's dialogue.

"Talk about a lifesaver! Mac was the answer to my prayers. Come on back to my office and I will fill you in on all the details."

When all three had taken their seats around Robert's conference table, he began. "As Mac has probably already told you, I am a High I. I am people oriented and shy away from the details of business. I'm much better today, but I still have to work on staying with the details. Before, I seldom wrote anything down and would try to keep my thoughts organized in my head. I was planning on the go without input from anyone in the company.

"About two o'clock one afternoon, which is my normal lunch-time, I was eating a sandwich at the local deli when Mac sat down next to me at the counter. I was reading the sports page and looked up when he grabbed a menu. As is typical for me, I introduced myself and mentioned to Mac that I hadn't seen him eating here. He said he was new to town and we talked about business. I couldn't help but notice he was a carpenter, so I asked him if he'd like to walk back to the store.

"By the time we entered the front door Mac seemed to know my life's story. I didn't fully understand then how much he already knew about my business, and me but I was drawn to him like a magnet. I kept saying to myself, this mysterious man has a great deal of knowl-edge—and I couldn't help but to listen to him.

"When the subject of meetings came up that's when he really had my attention. He patiently listened while I tried to explain my dilem-ma, and when I finished he reached into his toolbox and handed me this small egg timer in the shape of an hourglass."

Holding the timer up from its corner on his desk, Robert continued, "This is to remind me to begin and end meetings on time. It also indicates that I should have an agenda and distribute it in plenty of time prior the meeting so all participants can be prepared. I should also schedule meetings in advance so everyone involved can make arrangements to attend.

"This turned out to be a great start. Our meetings and planning improved. My frustration ebbed—but that was only until the fifth store was opened. By that time our staff was so large I had to stop micromanaging, a principle Mac explained but one I didn't pick up right away. It was during his second visit that we reevaluated the meetings and developed this schedule."

Robert pulled a calendar off his desk along with what looked like a manual. "This is our administrative manual with all the action plans that apply to the administration and office functions. Here is a recap of our scheduling:

"Daily meetings are held at six forty-five a.m. We call these our daily huddles, and they last a maximum of eight minutes, or one minute per attendee. This time is important because we open the doors at seven so we have to be finished to begin the day. During the eight minutes we review in bullet point format our daily activity. We don't even sit down, but it's a great opportunity to check in; if anyone needs help they get together after the daily huddle. If someone is missing, we continue without them.

"Our weekly meetings are on Wednesdays at eight a.m. These last between an hour and an hour and a half, tops. We review our weekly activities and keep an eye on the traffic light."

Gregg couldn't wait to ask, "Traffic light?"

Robert nodded. "Think of it as an indicator of the status of our activities. Red indicates that we are in danger of not achieving our goal or we are behind schedule. Yellow specifies we are okay but to use caution and don't take those activities for granted. Green is the one we all look for. It shows we are close to accomplishing our objective, there are no glitches, and there is high possibility we will be ahead of schedule.

"The weekly meeting consists of three phases. Phase 1 is when we give the flash reports. These, too, are in bullet point format, allowing each person to list the highlights of their week's activities and plans, which are then jotted down on a board. Next to each highlight on the board is a color indicator showing the status of each. Based on what's written and what colors are marked, we refine our agenda.

"The agenda, or Phase 2, consists of the topics that require discussion and are listed in priority as agreed upon by the group. Only tactical items go in this agenda. I know Mac has already explained the action planning process; therefore, think of these as the What. The How, Who, and When are not included at this time. These are added later at a second meeting or breakout session with the critical people attending.

"Phase 3 takes place after the Whats are listed. Only those items that can be addressed during these weekly meetings and have adequate information to make a decision are placed in Phase 3. Others that cannot be attended to are included in the following week's flash report."

Robert paused to let Gregg finish scribbling in his notebook. "The strategic planning meeting is held on a monthly basis. We work on the immediate strategic issues that may have changed since our annual strategic off-site planning session. We will discuss at this monthly gathering changes in our marketing and sales plan due to competitive moves or changes in the economy, or issues that may come up in operations or accounting and administration issues. We will extend the time based on the circumstances or degree of urgency.

"Gregg, imagine these meetings like newscasts. The daily huddle is like CNN Headline News. The weekly is the hour-long news in prime time. The monthly is a full in-depth news program as you might see on a Sunday morning. They all have a purpose to fit a specific planning need."

Gregg finished up with his notes, fascinated by Robert's explanation as well as the stubby yellow pencil that stayed constantly sharp. "Robert, that was indeed helpful. I understand the idea, but I know I will have to go back to practice this and the other useful concepts Mac has introduced."

Robert handed Gregg a document across the table. "Here's a copy of what we use as our meeting criteria throughout the company, including our annual off-site strategic meeting. These guidelines will be very beneficial when you return to work and put them to use."

Gregg took the pages from Robert and read:

Meeting Criteria

The concept of holding productive meetings is to limit their duration and include only those at a specific level of management. The following format is designed for top executives but is applicable for all management and supervisory levels.

Daily Meeting (Huddles)

Daily meetings are held at a specific time each morning and include only key individuals of the company. Each participant is allowed up to two minutes to discuss the highlights of their day giving only the "bullet points" or a one- or two-sentence description. The intention is not to make any decisions but to keep the other key players informed of that day's activities. If input or support is needed from one or more of the other participates, then a time is agreed upon to discuss that topic later in the day. Notes and calendars are used to ensure the critical issues are not omitted and any necessary appointments are confirmed.

If one participant is unable to attend a daily meeting or unable to connect to a conference call, the others will continue as above. This daily meeting should be held with everyone standing to emphasis its brevity and minimize unnecessary conversations.

WEEKLY MEETING

Weekly meetings are held on a specific day of the week and are limited to a maximum of ninety minutes. The first part of the meeting allows each person to give a "flash report" of the week's major activities and plans. Each participant writes on a board a five- to eight-word description of the activity or plan.

Next, the group reviews each topic and places a color indicating its importance for discussion at this weekly meeting. Think of a traffic light. Red is most pressing and might relate to the timing of an event, such as falling behind in the schedule of the activity or being in danger of not achieving a goal. Yellow indicates caution, not to take the activity or plan for granted, and outlining steps required to keep the indicator light from turning red. Green implies the topic is on target and on schedule, and that there is assurance the goal will be met or exceeded.

Based on the activity, plan, or topic, and the color indicator, an agenda is created for that weekly meeting beginning with red. Only tactical items are discussed—these are the What. The How, Who, and When are addressed at another agreed upon time when all the individuals needed are in attendance.

Only those items having adequate information to make a decision are addressed during this weekly meeting. Other issues that cannot be attended to are included in the following week's flash report, or another time is scheduled based on the circumstances and urgency. Any strategic issues are included in the monthly meeting.

Monthly Meeting

The monthly meeting or strategic planning session is designed to discuss the strategic issues of the company or organization. It is best held at the same time and day each month after the monthly financials are distributed. The monthly meeting is in lieu of a weekly meeting. Items to be included are those that may alter the annual strategic plan or have a mid- to long-term impact on the budget.

Adding a new product recently introduced, opening up a new territory earlier than anticipated, closing a facility, or an unexpected capital expenditures are examples of strategic issues.

Strategic Meeting

Once a year, a strategic meeting is held off-site to evaluate the current year's performance against budget and create a strategic or business plan for the coming year. Each participant prepares in detail their presentation with copies to be distributed to each individual along with supporting financials. From this input, the company's business plan for next year is drafted, and the accountable financial person develops a projected budget to include the profit and loss statement, balance sheet, and cash flow statement. This meeting is scheduled far enough in advance so the business plan and budget agreed upon at this off-site meeting can be distributed prior to the beginning of the next fiscal year.

This eliminates a lack of planning for the first several months of the new fiscal year and increases productivity for the first fiscal quarter.

Gregg felt an urge to immediately begin applying what he had learned. He sensed an underlying drive to improve his life and the lives of others. And he vowed come hell or high water was going to do it. He could feel his pulse racing as they said their good-byes to Robert and he climbed back into the red truck with Mac. He decided to review the notes he had taken to try and focus his thoughts.

He was in the middle of sorting everything out in his head when he had the sensation the pickup was slowing down. He glanced over to the speedometer, which indicated they were moving at thirty miles an hour. When he looked out the window, the scenery was passing at what he perceived to be that same speed. At second glance, he realized he was back in his neighborhood.

He had known it was to be the last visit, but he felt disappointed. "Are we home?"

Mac nodded. "Yes, Gregg, we have had a pretty full morning."

It had been full; it had been as full as an entire day. But instead of feeling tired and discouraged as they pulled up in his driveway, Gregg felt energized. "Mac, I cannot begin to tell you how much I appreciate what you have done for me," he said. "I know in the beginning I was a real pain. You have to admit that when you suddenly appeared in my bathroom it was a little unnerving. Now I can see the value of my trip with you and especially hearing how all your friends applied the lessons you shared with them."

Putting the pickup in park, Mac reached out a friendly hand and placed it on Gregg's shoulder. "You've been exposed to a great deal of information, and with your High D behavior style you will want to do it all in one day. Take your time and you will absorb it. Set yourself and your staff up for success, not failure. Do things right the first time." He patted Gregg's shoulder for emphasis. "What you've seen and heard is not meant to be a project. It is a process! It'll take some time to work out the bugs, but it will change lives, beginning with yours. You must continue to use what you've learned and improve upon it as you would in mastering any other skill."

Gregg laughed a little at how well Mac knew him. "Don't worry, I fully understand I have to practice to become proficient. I want to be a better person, communicate more efficiently, and be a respected leader. I want all those who work for me—no, work with me—to be the best they can be. I have the motivation to implement these lessons. I am the owner of my issues, and I will be the owner of how I resolve them. I have the tools you gave me as reminders."

Mac reached for his toolbox. "Gregg, I have one more tool to give you. I want you to take this."

Gregg watched him open the toolbox and pull out the oldest Mickey Mouse alarm clock he had ever seen. There was Mickey on the dial with his yellow hands pointing to six fifteen and two brass bells on top of the clock serving as the alarm.

"Take this clock to your office and place it on your desk."

Puzzled by Mac's request Gregg said, "I have a digital brass clock that keeps excellent time. Why do I need this?"

"This alarm clock has special properties," Mac said with a wink. "Besides keeping the most accurate time, you can use it to recreate any past situations in your business that didn't go well."

Gregg knew by now to listen to his mentor and waited patiently for Mac to explain.

"When you recall an event or situation that didn't turn out the way you wanted, press the alarm button on the Mickey Mouse clock. It will take you back to that precise moment and you can handle the same circumstances using the new knowledge you have. You'll be able to compare the before with the after behavior and watch the differences in outcome; this will be a wonderful learning experience. Try it a few times and you'll be ready to enter into a much more pleasurable business world. I know you'll find your business to be fun and you will be able to impact the lives of all those individuals who cross your path."

Stunned, Gregg took the clock. "Mac, I don't know how to thank you."

Mac smiled. "I'll tell you how. Use what you've learned and recreate your company so it will become what you have always wished it to be. Spend time with your family and be the husband and father they have wanted and needed."

Gregg looked at Mac and their eyes locked. The message was clear and unspoken. Mac said, "You'll feel a bit disoriented when you leave the truck. Splash some water on your face and you'll feel better instantly. I promise."

Gregg shook the carpenter's hand and repeated his thanks. Mac said, "Now that you've been on a trip and visited my friends, you're one of us—and I always keep an eye on my friends. I'll be with you and provide you with insights, but I appear only if and when I am needed. Go practice what you have learned."

Gregg opened the door of the pickup. And...

Chapter 10

With both hands Gregg grabbed the sides of the sink. He felt disoriented and instinctively splashed water on his head and face. Looking in the mirror, he noticed there were a few streaks of shaving lather remaining on his cheeks and neck and wiped them off with his towel.

He felt as if he had awakened from a dream. As his head cleared, he looked at his reflection and saw an energized face and eyes that were eager to begin the day. Smiling to himself, he savored this astonishing new feeling. Mac was right: this was going to be a new beginning. Yes, indeed!

After dressing and putting on his favorite tie, Gregg bounded down the flight of steps to the kitchen. Elaine had gotten up and was preparing breakfast and the kids' lunches. He walked over to her and gave her the usual morning kiss, but this time it lingered a bit longer.

When she opened her dark brown eyes they were surprised and pleased. "What has gotten into you this morning?" she teased.

Gregg shrugged happily. "It's such a beautiful day and I feel amazing."

"Well, whatever it is don't lose it during the day," she said, giving him a wink.

Gregg sat down and ate breakfast with his kids, something he had not done in quite a while. He engaged them in conversation and showed a real interest in Cristina's upcoming soccer match and Lucy's participation in the fifth grade art exhibit. The morning paper remained unread on the counter. When they finished eating he gave each of his family a kiss on the forehead and told them how much he loved them. Then, grabbing his briefcase, he waved goodbye and bounced out of the kitchen for the beginning of a truly new day and a new life.

On his way out the door, he heard Cristina say to her mom, "What happened to Dad? I think he's been hit over the head."

As Gregg settled into the driver's seat his hands were not gripping the steering wheel. He left at his normal time of six forty and began the twenty-minute drive to the office, but without trying to beat the yellow lights or becoming irritated with the other commuters. He kept within the speed limit and to his surprise pulled into his parking space five minutes earlier than usual.

Passing the maintenance crew cleaning the area in front of the office, Gregg saw Johnson Rivers meticulously wiping one of the front glass doors and paused. "Johnson, have I told you lately that you and your crew do an outstanding job and how much I appreciate all the years you have spent with the company?"

Johnson paused and scrutinized his employer for a moment. Then he replied, "No, Mr. Gregg, I can't say you have. But thanks."

As he continued on, Gregg could see Johnson's reflection in the window. He was shaking his head in wonderment.

The warehouse had already opened for the morning deliveries but the office was still vacant. He had at least forty minutes "to practice," as Mac had instructed, before anyone arrived. But where to begin?

He placed the Mickey Mouse clock on his desk next to the digital one. Both showed the exact same time. Gregg leaned back in his chair and closed his eyes, trying to imagine an incident he could use.

As images spun around in his head, he suddenly remembered events of a month ago. He had just told Mike that the company had finally won over Rob Cummings, a major tool distributor, and Gregg had signed an agreement to distribute Rob's products which would complete an assortment of goods that had been missing from his company's inventory. Cummings was a stickler for details and did not deviate from his published criteria for distribution. His number one rule for the distributors handling Cummings Tools was that they maintain their pricing structure. As Gregg was leaving Mike's office, he had called over his shoulder reminding the VP not to cut prices and stick by the rules.

Next he had gone to the warehouse to handle another essential request from Rob: to support the launch of Cummings' latest tool in the southeast territory that was assigned to Herbert and Associates. The marketing strategy was to offer the new pneumatic drill at no cost to the retailers when the distributor filled the next order. Cummings had experienced for years that the best way to promote and sell a new product was to put it literally into the hands of those selling it. When the retailer understood the ease of use and the efficiency of one of the new devices, the chances of its success greatly increased. It was to be marked to the attention of a specific individual at each retail company along with an instructional DVD. This was a follow-up to the original sales presentation as a goodwill gesture on behalf of Cummings. These drills were expensive, and Gregg wanted to make sure George in operations got the message from him personally.

But as he had been explaining the details to the warehouse manager, he was paged for an important call. As the situation played out now in Gregg's mind, he realized he had never returned to George to finish the instructions.

He put his head in his hands as these two episodes became clear. Now he was beginning to realize why his company had almost lost the Cummings line. Within two weeks of signing the agreement he had received a furious call from Rob. Mike had approved a ten percent price reduction for one of the company's best customers, and none of the demonstration drills had been included in the orders.

Gregg had to pull every string he had, calling in all his markers to remain the Cummings distributor for the southeast. Now he saw that the whole scenario could have been avoided. Opening his eyes and looking up, he again spotted Mickey Mouse pointing to the time of day.

"Well, Mickey, let's see what happens," he said to an empty office and tapped the button on top of the clock as Mac had instructed.

Gregg was suddenly standing outside Mike's office. Disoriented, he thought, *Now I know how Captain Kirk must have felt*. He glanced at the peel-off calendar on the wall next to Mike's door; the date was one month earlier. His sales VP was on the phone as he entered. Mike completed his conversation and greeted Gregg with his stale but standard questions. "How's it going? What's new in this world of ours?"

"I have great news for you, but it's important that we talk," Gregg informed him.

"Shoot. I'm just going to check my e-mail."

"No, Mike, I'd really like your full attention. When you finish please drop by my office and I will bring you up to date."

Mike looked startled, but nodded his agreement as Gregg left.

Gregg realized as he returned to his office this was a completely new approach. In the past he probably would have talked to Mike while his VP of Sales was on the computer. *If eighty percent of what is said is misunderstood, I wonder how Mac would have calculated this percentage with my talking to Mike while he was preoccupied,* he thought.

Back at his office Gregg phoned George to meet with Mike and him. When his they arrived, he asked out of curiosity, though he already knew the answer, "Do either of you have anything to write with and some paper?"

He received looks from the two men as if he had asked them to loan him a million dollars. "Here is a pad and pencil for each of you," Gregg said handing them out. "I think you need to take some notes. Communications can improve thirty percent if we simply take the time to write down the details."

Mike and George exchanged concerned looks, but they dutifully took the paper and pencils and sat down.

Gregg paused until the two were ready and he had their attention. He was amused at their reaction to him. "I've met with Rob Cummings, and we have signed an agreement to distribute his tools in all of our territories."

Mike hopped up and pumped his hand in the air, giving a loud "Hot damn!" George remained seated but with a wide grin on his face, half at Mike's response and half at the good news.

When Mike sat down again, Gregg continued. "As you both know, this is a vital account both in volume and in profits. To protect the margins I have agreed to Rob's request that there will be no price cutting on any of his products. Mike, I want you to review all of the Cummings' orders and check for proper pricing prior to George filling the order. George, instruct your men that if Mike's initials are not on the order, it is not to be filled." He paused, raising his eyebrows and glancing at their pads. George picked up his pencil and began to scribble down notes. Mike only tapped the eraser on the pad in an excited rhythm.

"George, as part of the Cummings kickoff promotion we are to pack one new pneumatic drill in the next order to each retailer. You have to keep up with these allocations to ensure only one goes to each retailer selling the Cummings line. It also must be addressed to the individual who attended the original sales presentation by Cummings. I have a list of those names.

"Mike, I want you to follow up with the regional managers on the details so they can pass them along to the reps."

Gregg watched George taking notes while Mike's pencil never touched the page. "Mike, how are you going to remember these instructions?" he asked.

Tapping the side of his head Mike responded seriously, "You know I have a mind like an elephant."

"I know you do, but humor me and take a minute or two to write down the points we covered," instructed Gregg.

Mike gave him a puzzled look but did as he was asked. When finished he looked up and waited.

"Please read your notes back to make sure we are all in concurrence," Gregg requested.

Mike said confidently, "First, we are handling the Cummings account. We have to maintain the price, and I must approve any price deviations as we do with the other accounts. My initials go on the orders so George can ship them."

Gregg was fuming but heard a whisper to keep his composure. It sounded like Mac's voice. "Mike, why did you say you must approve any price changes?" *Good*, he thought. *Now I have Mike thinking instead of me reacting. But he's got to improve his listening skills.*

"That's the way we've always done it. I just assumed we would handle the account like all the others."

Okay, Gregg said to himself. *This will be my first test as a coach. I have to be accountable for my communications and not blame Mike for not absorbing the facts. Now, what do I do?*

Again, he heard a whisper.

Leaning forward in his chair for emphasis, he said, "Mike, I signed an agreement with Rob to protect his pricing. We cannot deviate from the pricing structure at all, or we will lose the line."

Mike's brow furrowed. "You gotta to be kidding!"

Gregg continued, "No, I'm serious. That's the only way Cummings does business. I need you to help me maintain the pricing policy and make sure no order goes to George with any deviations at all. Now, what do the three of us need to do to make this happen?"

"I'm having a conference call later with the regional managers," Mike informed him. "I'll tell them about maintaining prices."

"Can you write a memo to them, e-mail the explanation of the rules, and address any questions during the call?" asked Gregg.

"Sure. No problem," Mike replied, rubbing his chin, baffled at Gregg's intensity.

Gregg was pleased to hear George add, "And Mike, if you will send all the Cummings orders to me instead of to the warehouse, I'll double check the pricing. Gregg, I'll inform Tom of this discussion. He checks my mailbox when I'm not available and will work with me to ensure the drills are sent out on time and to the right individuals."

As Mike and George left, Gregg pushed the top of the Mickey alarm clock and found himself back in the present. He couldn't help but smile as he saw that Mickey's hand had only moved fifteen minutes. *Could it be that if I had spent time all along with Mike and George,*

I would have saved countless hours and a ton of stress? I'll never let that happen to me in the future. Improving communication and listening skills had moved to the top of his list, and he planned to make sure it was also a company priority. Now, what about the monthly sales meeting when they had been discussing sales goals? Again he pushed the button on the alarm clock.

He found himself in the conference room the "previous Monday." Waiting were his three regional sales managers under Mike. Again he started the discussion with Jon, the sales rep for Georgia and the Carolinas. Jon explained that not only had he reached his sales targets, he had exceeded them.

Gregg remembered that he had wasted thirty minutes arguing with Jon about his goals, which absolutely would not be the case this time. Two of the other managers sat idly, their minds somewhere else. Gregg had all the numbers in front of him and the company was behind, not ahead of, the sales goal. Mac's picture of the assumption gap appeared mentally, and the staff meeting resumed.

Gregg began his reenactment of the previous meeting using his recently acquired knowledge. "I want to review our sales status and how we are comparing with the plan," he began. "I would like each of you to bring me up to date with your month's budget compared to actual figures for your territory."

Jon was the first to respond. "I am glad to say my territory has exceeded our goal by nine percent for the month. If what I've got in the works develops, the trend will increase for the remainder of the quarter."

Instead of focusing on Jon, Gregg moved on to the other managers. "How about you, Blake, what are your results?"

"Gee, Gregg, I didn't know you wanted the details. I'm afraid I'm not prepared."

"And Jeff, fill us in?"

Jeff, the manager for the remaining southeastern states pulled an envelope from his pocket and read from the back. "Looks like Florida is okay but we need to work on the other two states," he told the group.

How could this be? Gregg asked himself. He'd had no idea these guys were not better prepared and weren't giving adequate attention to their sales reports. *I don't even want to know how long this has been taking place,* he thought, shaking his head. Just then, he heard like a whisper in his ear: "Close the assumption gap."

He spoke up. "I've been giving a great deal of thought to the way the company is being managed, and I mean starting with me. I know we can be more productive, but we have to be properly informed, and to do that we need accurate and timely information. I know this is unusual, but I'd like you all to return this month for another meeting that will include Mike and Sally. Sally as controller works with the numbers daily and can help us with understanding our progress. As usual, you're responsible for your reps' travel arrangements to get to this meeting. When you get the details from Mike, please pass them along to all of your reps. I want everybody to be present."

Gregg got up and closed the meeting. He pressed Mickey's button again and came back to the present. *This assuming has to stop!* he said to himself. *I had no idea how unprepared the reps are.* He was suddenly bombarded with questions and thoughts. *What has Mike been doing? I wonder if he has any better knowledge of the figures. Why wasn't he attending that meeting?* Gregg made another note to himself to follow up with Mike. He wasn't going to trust his memory. *Maybe I should invest in a PDA to keep up with my notes and schedule.*

Gregg suddenly saw the stubby yellow pencil beside his notepad. How had it found its way in here? It was still sharp, so he used it to write down other reminders, including a note to hold a meeting with Mike and the reps and Sally. He could feel himself changing and surging with new energy.

Then, instead of hollering for his secretary to come in, Gregg picked up his intercom. "Nancy, could you come in with your pad?"

She entered the office with a dumbfounded look. "What's wrong?" she asked. "Are you okay?"

"We need to talk."

Before he could continue, Nancy interrupted, "Am I getting fired?"

"No!" Gregg reassured her hastily. "No, Nancy, you are doing a good job—but I want both of us to do an excellent job and I need your help. Please, sit down."

Nancy complied. "How can I help you?"

"Let's start with you reminding me of your background and qualifications."

Momentarily confused, she began, "I was the administrative assistant for two vice presidents at my previous company. I ran their offices and took care of the details when they traveled, which was most of the time. I scheduled meetings, made travel arrangements, handled all correspondence, filled out the expense reports, and answered their e-mails and phone calls. I also—"

"Why do you not do the same things here?" interrupted Gregg.

"You won't let me!" Nancy blurted out, then held her hand to her mouth. "I'm sorry," she said looking down at her lap.

Gregg leaned forward. "Nancy, I should be the one to apologize, not you. You are a very talented administrative assistant, but I have been treating you like an entry-level secretary straight out of school. I'm sure you never learned to mind read, and I haven't learned to listen very well. That doesn't make for a very good combination. You've been telling me for years to allow you to handle more of my work. I didn't have my third ear tuned in."

"I'm not following you," Nancy said slowly.

Gregg sat back in his chair, a small smile on his face. "I want to tell you about a dream I had last night. It may sound a little extreme but when I awoke I began to change my outlook on life and how I must improve this business. It all begins with me, and that's where you come in."

Gregg related the highlights of his encounter with Mac. "So I want to be a better listener. I want to use the three ears I learned about in the dream, especially the one that helps me to understand what others want to say but do not know how or are reluctant to express. I want to improve our planning and communications, and I want to be more of a strategic thinker. We've got to get out of this crisis environment and become more proactive. I want to delegate better and align the circles."

"Hold on," Nancy cautioned. "I need to take some notes." She hurried to her desk and returned with her pad. Then she asked, "How can I really help you? You always want to do things yourself. There are so many activities I think I can do, but I haven't had the opportunity to master any of them."

Gregg gestured with a flourish. "That's why as of today you are my official administrative assistant. The first item on this agenda is for us to write a job description for you. We will start there and I will work with you to understand my expectations of your work and how I can develop you so we'll both be comfortable with your new position."

"Are you serious?" Nancy asked.

"Of course, why do you ask?"

She looked overwhelmed. "I've longed for this to take place but I gave up years ago. To be perfectly honest with you, I have touched up my resume and I plan to look for another position."

"Thank goodness for my dream," Gregg said earnestly. "It would be a shame for you to leave at this time. What do you need from me for you to remain with the company?" He hoped he had caught the situation in time.

"Only a commitment that you will do what you said earlier."

Gregg leaned forward. "If I don't then you should definitely leave, because without this commitment I run the risk of losing the whole company. Remember in the dream I told you about the 'want to's' and how important it is to be an owner of issues and solutions? Well, I am the owner of this working relationship, and I am committed."

"Where do we begin?" asked Nancy with anticipation.

"Do I have your 'want to' to be my administrative assistant?"

"Oh, yes. I cannot tell you how excited I am," she declared. "I won't disappoint you."

"Okay. The first thing I need you to do is schedule a meeting next Monday with Mike, the regional managers, and Sally to discuss the results of the last two months. We'll need three rooms for the managers. See what the conference center has available and get back to me."

Gregg paused, allowing Nancy to catch up with her writing. Then he said, "And I am delighted that you are staying and taking the new position. Now, be sure to start on that job description, and we'll discuss your draft and come up with a final one together."

He expected Nancy to leave, but she remained in the chair. "I was anticipating the sales meeting with Mike and the others. How long will it last? What will they need to bring? Do you require a flip chart or your PowerPoint projector and screen?"

Gregg was impressed. This was the kind of teamwork that would move them forward. "Great thinking. The meeting will not last over an hour and half. Each manager should bring their individual reports and Sally should bring—no, ask her if she can join me now so I can discuss with her what she thinks we need."

Nancy began to return to her office when Gregg added, "Please join Sally and me. I want you to hear what she has to say so we can be better prepared."

"Aye, aye, sir." She saluted jovially. Then, "Isn't it a beautiful day?" she said to no one in particular.

Gregg answered under his breath, "It certainly is."

Chapter 11

At seven forty-five a.m., Sally knocked on Gregg's door and walked into his office. "Nancy said you would like to see me," she said, concern written all over her face.

Gregg smiled to put her at ease. "Please, sit down. I need your help and would like to have a discussion with you."

"What's wrong, are you in bankruptcy?" Sally asked sitting on the edge of her chair, staring at Gregg as if waiting for the other shoe to drop.

Have I really caused this much anxiety within the company? Gregg thought, astonished at her response. Here Nancy thought she was being fired, and now Sally wanted to know if the company was in bankruptcy. *Boy, do I have my work cut out for me.* But Rome hadn't been built in a day, so he figured there was nothing wrong with this process taking some time.

You're committed and you are the owner, suddenly registered in his consciousness.

Sally was looking at him inquiringly.

"No, Sally, it's nothing like that," he responded. "I want to have a meeting with Mike and all the regional sales managers. I'm disappointed in their performance, but I need you to help me understand the numbers and everything that we have to do to ensure Mike and the managers know what they are dealing with when it comes to budgets and financials. I believe they aren't taking this seriously because they don't know how to interpret the figures. I bet if they were honest they would say it was like trying to understand a different language."

Sally let out a long sigh. "Did you sleep okay last night?" she asked.

Gregg was beginning to accept these remarks in stride, and was both amused and grateful. "Thank you for your concern, but I'm fine. I've been doing some thinking about the company and talking to other businesses. For the first time in a long while I am considering some new ideas—at least, new to me."

Sally began to look interested as he continued, "For starters, I want to create a budget that is actionable, timely, and understood by those in mid-management and the executive team. I want everyone in this group to know how they can create value for the company, as well as what is required to impact the bottom line either by adding revenues and profits or reducing overhead and expenses. I want to start with the sales managers and Mike. Will you help?"

Sally hesitated. "Gregg, I was coming in this morning to tell you I am leaving the company. I will give you a month's notice, though, and help in any way I can prior to my departure."

Gregg felt a sinking feeling in the pit of his stomach. Sally had always done an excellent job and he'd had no indication of her dissatisfaction. *It must be her salary. I knew I should have given her a raise.*

Then came a murmur in his ear: *Remember, you first need to listen to understand before talking to be understood.* Maybe there was more to it.

"What has led to your decision?" he asked. "I didn't realize you were so unhappy with the company. You've been here for over ten years."

Sally leaned forward earnestly. "I love Herbert and Associates, and because I do I leave each day a little more frustrated. There is so much potential here, but I have my doubts as to the company's future. With all the time and effort spent, we should be much more profitable and not always in a cash bind. I haven't been able to communicate with you or the executive team in terms that any of you are willing to understand; maybe none of you are taking the financials seriously."

She hesitated, then plunged ahead. "Also, there are more excuses and finger pointing than any organization I have seen. All the negativism causes most of the long-term associates, the really loyal ones, to shut down. I have heard employees in the break room saying that if management doesn't care, why should they? The morale here is appalling. When there's an attitude like this, everyone gets down; they certainly cannot or will not be proactive. We are in one crisis after another, wasting time doing the same things over and over again but expecting different results. That's insane. It reminds me of an adage I once read: If I continue to do what I have always done, I will continue to get what I have always gotten." Sally appeared relieved to get this weight off her chest. Then she exhaled noisily "Gregg, I'm tired. I need a change."

Gregg knew she wasn't expecting him to respond well. He chose his words carefully. "You are absolutely right. I've known about the morale issue for some time; I just didn't want to face the truth. I appreciate your frankness."

Sally looked amazed. Then she said, "But why haven't you done something about it?" Voice rising, she continued, "It's your company. You're responsible for hundreds of lives, and it's not fair to any one of us. It is not fair to you." Her eyes were gleaming with moisture.

Gregg had a lump in his throat. He'd come in only a couple of hours ago happy as a kid at a birthday party. Now he felt like he could have been attending the funeral of a close friend. He was beginning to become dejected when he heard the keyboard of his computer making a noise. Turning to the computer screen he saw a message appear: YOU ARE THE OWNER. NOW TAKE CHARGE.

Sally hadn't noticed anything askew. Taking a deep breath, Gregg answered, "Again, you are accurate in your observations. I don't know how to make you believe me, but all of what you described is true and will be corrected."

Sally shook her head. "Gregg, I want to believe what you're saying. It's music to my ears. But how many times have we had this same discussion? At least your response is more positive, that I can say. But you've been putting me off with excuses and empty promises for years."

Gregg hesitated, but desperate times called for desperate measures. "Sally, I must tell you about a dream I had last night. Please listen to the complete story before asking questions." He gave an abbreviated version of his "trip" with Mac and his encounters. When he finished there was utter silence.

Gregg finally broke it. "You said you would give a month's notice. Allow me that month to prove my sincerity and observe the changes that will take place. I am going to put your notice on hold and would like you to participate in the meeting with the sales managers."

Slowly, Sally nodded in agreement. "What do you need me to prepare for your discussion?"

"A football." He suppressed a chuckle at her blank expression. "I know that means nothing now, but hear me out. We've lost the basics of running a business. Blocking and tackling are not the fundamentals to be addressed. We need to know the very game we are playing. That is the football.

"Sally, we have to define this business. What are we and what do we want to be? What is our purpose? Why are we in business? Who are our customers and what do we provide them? What do the customers think of us? Where are we going?" Gregg asked urgently, emphasizing with his hands, trying to get through to her.

For the next half an hour they composed an agenda and listed the materials the regional managers needed for the meeting the next week. Nancy would e-mail it to each one and follow it up with a phone call. With Sally's input they made a list of questions for the staff. The last sentence of the e-mail reminded the managers to write down a list of all the issues or problems they were experiencing within the company. Nancy would have these instructions ready for Gregg at the nine o'clock staff meeting with Mike, George, and Sally.

Gregg knew he was pushing hard to take action. Time was against him, and his staff and the other managers were always waiting until the last minute to collect their thoughts and prepare.

For once, he was on time to the staff meeting and had the memo for the next meeting ready. He wished he'd had more time to prepare, as he typically adlibbed while planning the remainder of the meeting while he was talking. But that was going to stop as well. He was beginning to sense events before they happened. He knew Sally would be on time but that the others would straggle in as he had frequently done. And why should they be on time when he typically wasn't? Gregg knew he had set the wrong example.

It was 9:06 when Mike walked in and noticed both Gregg and Nancy waiting patiently in their places. Five minutes later George joined the group. "Oops, I must be late."

It was Gregg's intuition they were late not only because he typically was, but also because he often lambasted them for most anything that was not to his liking. A thought flashed through his head that he was not mad at these three; rather, he was angry with himself and simply took out his frustrations on the others.

When everyone was comfortable and he had their attention, he stood up, something he had never done before. "We have a crisis on our hands," he said, pausing to allow the words to register. "I remember a comic strip titled 'Pogo' that my dad loved to read. His favorite line from one strip was, 'I have met the enemy and it is me.' The same holds true today; we are the crisis. We are the enemy."

Gregg searched their faces and deferred his response to their rebuttals.

"How can you say that?" George sounded hurt.

"I take that as a personal insult," Mike protested testily.

Gregg paused to make sure they were done. "Sally, would you like to add anything?"

"Only what you have said is the truth and should have been said years ago." The look on her face said clearly, *What have I got to lose?*

Gregg took control again and continued, "How would each of you describe our year-to-date performance?"

After a very long pause Mike said, "Sales are on target and we now have the Cummings line, which has been our goal for years."

George followed, "There have been fifty-six accident free days in the warehouse, and OSHA gave us a good rating."

"Sally?" Gregg prompted again.

"Where do I begin? For starters, our cash flow is inadequate to service the debt, we are barely paying the bills, and twice we have been close to not making payroll deadlines. Our current ratio is poor, debt to equity is awful, and EBITDA is down the tubes."

Gregg took over the conversation before Mike or George could voice their shock. "I want to be honest with all of you, and vice versa. Who understands fully what Sally just told us? I will start by saying I don't. I've discussed bits and pieces with her, but I don't begin to comprehend the significance of the ratios. I can't even define EBITDA, much less calculate it."

Mike and George both confirmed their lack of knowledge in these areas. Sitting down, Gregg continued calmly, "I am asking your forgiveness for my lack of leadership and not taking the lead in our development. I am also requesting that each one of us be accountable to the others by beginning this very moment to right our wrongs of the past. I want all of us to forget the past and concentrate on the present. I've met with Sally earlier, and we have created a working document to come together in a common cause. I would like to call it our Unity of Purpose, and I'd like to meet again after you've had some time to look over it.

"Sally, please explain the purpose of this meeting and what we need in order to be prepared."

Sally went into detail, covering each question on the memo and telling Gregg, Mike, and George what to bring. "I will have the financials and budgets, and I'll develop some worksheets to aid your understanding of the significance of the figures. We'll spend some time on definitions and the basic concepts. As Gregg said to me, we must drill down even below the fundamentals." She smiled at him briefly. "I'm not much of a football enthusiast, but using Gregg's example, before we start to work on blocking and tackling, we are going to first understand the game we are playing. Gregg, I thought more about your comment this morning. The football is symbolic of the game we are playing; if we don't know what the game is, how in the world can we work on the fundamentals? In our case, the football is the very business life of Herbert and Associates."

Then Gregg covered a few other minor topics. "We are going to cut this meeting short and reconvene again this afternoon. Think about what I've said. We are beginning a new and exciting chapter in our business lives. Any questions?"

He was met with stunned silence. Then Sally asked Mike and George to remain so she could cover some of the basics for their next meeting, and Gregg headed to his ten o'clock orientation of new employees. His energy was high and he was pumped about meeting the newest members of his staff. In the past, he had given the new associates a short greeting and a cursory review of the beginnings of the company, and then promptly left. But not today.

When he arrived, Kristin, the HR Director, was taking care of some last minute paperwork. She looked up and introduced Gregg. "Everyone, I want you to meet the president of Herbert and Associates, Gregg Herbert."

Instead of marching up to the podium to begin his talk, Gregg walked around meeting each new employee and shaking their hands. Out of the corner of his eye he took in the expression on Kristin's face and smiled inwardly. *I hope I'm making a difference,* flashed through his mind.

When he was done greeting everyone, Gregg sat at a desk next to the others and told stories about how he'd started as a salesman and later bought the company. He added some humorous antidotes that Kristin had never heard before. As he was leaving, she stepped outside with him briefly and told him how much they all had appreciated his time. She even commented on how genuine he'd sounded. *I wonder what she meant by that remark,* Gregg thought as he headed back to his office.

Gregg spent the rest of the morning with Sally and Nancy and signed some checks even as he wondered what the bank balance was. He was about to check his e-mails and phone messages but suddenly stopped as if a great weight were pressing on him. Confused, he racked his brain as to the meaning of this "sign." *Okay, Mac, I know you are trying to tell me something. What is it?*

As he pondered this question Nancy came in with some more pink slips to add to his message pile. Now he knew!

"Nancy, let's review these e-mails and messages and see which ones you can handle. I'll take care of the rest." After a thorough twenty minutes of back and forth questions and answers, Nancy returned to her office with all but three calls. *Thanks, Mac,* was Gregg's simple acknowledgement.

The morning had flown by and now it was finally time to leave to meet Don Paulus for lunch. Instead of dreading the luncheon with the banker, Gregg now looked forward to their conversation. They had known each other for years and were as close as brothers. Both enjoyed playing on the rivalry of their alma maters and tried to get the best of each other on any occasion. It worked so well they always fell into the pattern of good-natured barbs quite naturally. Don's "How could I expect you to understand anything without a formal education? You poor devil, having to spend four years in reform school," was matched with Gregg's "It may have been, but at least I got a job. You had to go to graduate school before any employment came your way. And your boss was my classmate."

On the more somber side of life they had both been through tough personal issues and had stood by each other, lending their support in times of need.

Don was catching up on *The Wall Street Journal* as Gregg entered the club. They met there often, as it was a convenient place to have a conversation. Don put the paper down and looked at his watch.

"Damn, you're on time! A miracle! I know they didn't teach you how to tell time at that lowly place you call a university. I'm starved and it's your turn to buy. I think I saw steak as one of the specials."

As they enjoyed their meal and the accompanying banter, the conversation turned to business. Gregg started off. "Don, I've been giving a great deal of thought to the advice you've given me over the years. Concerns over my cash flow, not maximizing profits, borrowing for working capital and not paying off old debt have been expressed by you as problems numerous times. I just sloughed them off and lived in my world of denial. But it's time I faced the truth and dealt with these issues, and I need your help."

"Okay, what's the punch line?" Don joshed. Seeing the frown on Gregg's face, he sobered. "You don't even have to ask. What can I do?"

Gregg leaned back and prepared to tell his amazing story for the third time that day. "As you would say, I have had an epiphany." He told Don in minute detail of his encounter with Mac.

Don didn't interrupt; rather, he seemed captivated by the journey and the encounters. When Gregg completed the saga, he said, "I don't know what to say. I am totally at a loss for words."

"You're one of the few people I can tell all of the events that occurred," Gregg confided. "I simply said I had a dream to the others."

"Amazing! Gregg, what do you need from me? How can I help?" Don persisted.

"I want to sit down with you to understand what you look for as a banker when you review the financials. What should we work on to improve our financial picture? I talked to Sally this morning, as she has more knowledge in finance than I do; but I'd like you to check her qualifications and spend time with both of us."

Don gave him a big smile. "Gregg, it would be my pleasure not only as your friend but as your banker. You could have a great company, but you are nowhere close to the financial goals you should achieve. I have some ideas that could be beneficial."

"Check your calendar and we'll arrange a time for you, Sally and me to meet. You do know how to use a calendar?" Gregg asked mirthfully.

After a final exchange of volleys they said their goodbyes and Gregg returned to his office. He finished up the paperwork, met with his insurance agent, and began to tidy his desk. Just then, Nancy walked in.

"If we work on organizing your desk together, I can keep it that way," she suggested.

"An excellent idea," replied Gregg, and the two spent the next several hours straightening up. When they were finished, Gregg exclaimed, "I believe I can see the top of the desk. I didn't know it was brown."

Nancy couldn't help but laugh out loud.

"Nancy, thanks," Gregg said as she turned to leave.

"You are more than welcome," she replied.

"Time to go to the staff meeting," called Sally, peeking her head around the corner. She had a handful of folders. "What has happened to your desk? I never knew it had a top."

"Come on." Gregg gave her a mock frown. "Let's go, I've been picked on enough by Nancy. What do you have?"

"Only a start, but a good one," Sally said as they walked to the conference room. "This is the information I'm planning to go over next week. I'm really relieved to have a chance to discuss all of it with you,

Mike, and George first, however. You know, it's going to take more than one time to educate these guys on the basics of finance. I don't want to make them accountants, but for managers to manage effectively they must have the tools."

Sally began the meeting by dropping a bomb. "Last fiscal year we had record sales." She paused, giving each an opportunity to acknowledge Mike's efforts. "Our total sales were a little over twelve million—$12,578,967.05 to be exact." Again approving smiles were exchanged. "As you know, we have to pay for the products we sell, and what is left is our gross margin. From that figure we subtract selling, general and administration expenses." She looked around the room. "What would you guess was our net profit?"

Mike guessed six million while George estimated one and a half million. Sally raised her eyebrows. "How about $125,789.67—or, said another way, we spent $12,453,177.38 to generate $12,578,967.05 in sales. We made a whopping one percent net profit."

There was a shocked silence throughout the room.

"We have debt in excess of three million dollars," Sally continued. "Our inventory turns less than six times a year, and our accounts payable is close to four million. Receivables range from two to three million with too many accounts ninety days or older. Looking further at the balance sheet, our debt to equity is not quite one to one."

She continued, handing out the folders. "Our industry averages for net profit for businesses our size is 4.3 percent. That means our competitors are achieving four times the net profits we are. Our credit history is not good; therefore we are paying interest that is three points higher than our competitors'. The vendors do not give us the best deals; these are offered to others that pay their bills on time. And we aren't moving our inventory as fast as we should, so we're paying high interest for the luxury of having it in the warehouse even though we don't need all of it. We also pay additional insurance on that inventory and run a greater risk of damaging it before we send it out. When we took our physical inventory we found three hundred thousand more products than we had on the books. I guess it just grew on its own."

Sally finished handing out the folders and sat down. Mike was flipping through the papers as if dazed. Gregg had to admit to feeling overwhelmed as well. Taking a sip of water as if to reduce her frustration, Sally added, "We are serving as a bank to our customers. They aren't paying according to our terms, and we always accept some excuse as to why they cannot pay. Remember, we're paying high interest rates to carry these accounts. And one last point: the net worth or value of the company is slightly less than our total debts. Now do you get the picture, or better still, do you see our financial picture?"

No wonder she gave notice, thought Gregg. *Knowing and working with these figures would have frustrated anyone.*

Mike was first with a response. "Sally, I'm beginning to see what I haven't seen. I was focused on making the sales and letting the rest of you handle the other details because my old way of thinking was *it's not my job.* But if I'm to fill the shoes of a real VP of Sales, I must understand the fundaments of—no, the *football* of accounting. I need your help."

There was general acknowledgement of their need to learn. Sally had done an outstanding job in obtaining their attention, especially Mike, whom Gregg had expected to protest. There was an urgency and concern in her voice that carried over.

"When do we meet again?" Mike asked.

Gregg responded, "I think we can continue to have staff meetings every morning this week in order to prepare for the sales rep meeting on Monday. I'll see you tomorrow morning at nine a.m. just like today.

And as you put it, we will begin with the football of defining our business. If we don't know who we are or where we're going, we'll be totally lost—and we cannot afford that." He winked at Sally. She only stared back.

Gregg realized it would take more time for his team to grasp the concepts, but he was hoping they would become dedicated to learning how to be better leaders and managers. He hated to see Sally leave the company, though, especially knowing it was his own fault. This was a hard lesson for him and yet another reminder of the necessity of changing his mindset.

Walking back to his office, he told himself that, even with the last meeting and Sally's planned departure, this had been a great beginning. He felt like celebrating. Struck by sudden inspiration, he picked up his phone to call Elaine.

"Hi! How would you and the kids like to go out for dinner tonight?"

She sounded surprised. "But it's Monday and they have school tomorrow."

"I know, but I'll leave now so we can get something early. Come on, it'll be fun."

"Is this a continuation from this morning?" Elaine asked. "If it is, I like it. We'll be ready by the time you arrive home. Who knows, I may even have a special dessert for you," she said with a chuckle.

Gregg smiled as he hung up the phone. He was still smiling as he headed home. What a day!

Chapter 12

Elaine had spent a restless night. Raising her head, she moaned when she saw the green glow of the clock radio indicating four twenty-five a.m. Flashes of her married life had interrupted her sleep, creating a mental diary of the past twenty years.

She had known Gregg since they were children andhad dated him during high school and college.   But it would be several years after graduation when they met at a friend's wedding that they truly fell in love. The attraction was there for both, and after little over a year they decided to get married. At the time she'd felt like Cinderella and thought of Gregg as her Prince Charming. He was devoted to her and their two girls and provided them with love and more than the necessities. But as his business grew, he spent less time with his family. Talking to her girl friends, she learned they had similar concerns—that seemed to be life for couples in their forties and fifties.

As the business made more demands on Gregg's time, Elaine complained to him that she was competing for his attention, often accusing the business of being "the other woman" in his life. When the girls started school and began extracurricular activities, Elaine felt most of the time as if she were a single mom. Gregg's days at the office grew longer, and her weekends were lonelier. She knew she loved her husband, so she kept her thoughts to herself. But now Gregg's call inviting "his girls" to dinner and leaving work early to accommodate a school night had rekindled her longings for her "dream family."

Throughout her intermittent sleep she had been aware of being cradled in Gregg's arms, a closeness that had been lost over the last few years. This act of love now brought tears to her eyes, and she reached for a tissue.

"What's wrong?" Gregg said into the pillow.

With that question, years of frustration, anger, and hurt flooded over her along with the tears. Gregg held his wife and rocked her until she had exhausted her wave of emotions.

When she had quieted, he said, "Elaine, talk to me. Tell me."

"I realized at dinner with all of us together how much I missed those times. How much I've missed you." She started to cry again. "I have tried to be a good wife and support you and the business, but it's taken you away from us. Yesterday when you came down for breakfast, you were the Gregg that I remembered marrying. I caught myself reminiscing and having flashbacks of how things use to be, and I want them back so much," Elaine whispered between her sobs.

Gregg felt as if a knife had pierced his heart. "Elaine, I was thinking the exact same thing. I miss those times, too. You're right; I've become a slave to the business and it is managing me.

"I don't know if the dream I told you about was a dream or an out of body experience, but I truly don't care how I met Mac. I do know that he has changed my life and I will change ours."

Elaine wiped away a tear. "Oh, Gregg, I want to believe you, but we've had these talks so many times before. You do great for a few days and then there's always some crisis that pulls you back into the business and away from us."

Gregg chose his next words carefully. "You remember the sermon last Sunday about how the longest journey begins with the first step? I have taken that first step. I have begun the journey. I'm not sure where it'll lead me or how long it'll take to reach the destination, but I *will* make it. Hon, I really need you."

Elaine pulled away from him to look her husband in the eye. "Promise me that this is not idle talk and that our lives will change."

Gregg pictured Mac with his toolbox, saying he was not a carpenter that fixed things, but lives. He promised Elaine with a kiss.

They didn't go back to sleep but stayed awake discussing ways to accomplish their goals and reprioritize their time commitments. Then Gregg dressed for work and came down to share coffee with Elaine before the girls joined them for breakfast. She had made their favorite breakfast, which was usually reserved for Sundays.

Cristina was the first to the table. She exclaimed, "It's Tuesday, not Sunday! What's going on?" At sixteen she was becoming more aware of life's subtleties and didn't miss the changes in her parents' behavior. It wasn't the menu; it was the way they acted towards each other.

Lucy came down stairs and ran to Elaine. "Mommy, I can't get this ponytail to work." Elaine reached down and adjusted her daughter's hair adding a kiss.

"What's going on in that head of yours?" Gregg asked Cristina, noticing her frown.

"Just thinking."

"Do you care to share your thoughts?" inquired Elaine carefully.

Cristina took a deep breath. "I don't know what's really going on. Yesterday Dad acted strange, and today you both are weird. I hope it's not catching."

Her parents exchanged smiles and Elaine answered, "You are a very observant sixteen-year-old."

"Mom, you would have to be deaf and blind not to know something is changing. I just don't understand what has gotten into the two of you."

"For now let's just say our lives are changing for the better."

"That's no answer," protested Cristina.

"Okay, how's this?" Gregg offered. "I am changing my priorities in life. I'm going to spend more time with all of you—quality time. I'm learning how to help the people at work to do a better job, which will give me more time to be with my family."

All eyes were focused on Cristina. When she concentrated, her brow knitted and from the look on her face she was in deep thought. "That's great, Dad. But when I start dating I am not hanging out with you and Mom."

She seemed surprised when both her parents laughed.

Gregg arrived early at work for the staff meeting. He was anticipating a productive gathering, and his anticipation was heightened when he spotted his employees' cars already there. Maybe he had touched a nerve with them to begin on time.

When Gregg entered the meeting room he saw Mike and George enjoying the donuts that they picked up on the way to the office and Sally setting up the PowerPoint. *This is too good to be true!* he thought. *I guess I should be thankful for their efforts.* He greeted the group by saying, "Good morning, looks like another beautiful day."

Mike and George nodded with mouths full while Sally acknowledged, "Yes, it is, and I hope a most productive one." Gregg noticed she was actually smiling as she laid out the material.

Gregg passed on the donuts but grabbed a cup of coffee and removed the folder Sally had given to him from his briefcase as she began the meeting.

"I'll begin by reviewing some of the financial history of the company." Sally gave a brief but informative account of the past three years' activity, stressing again that although sales had trended upward the net profits had remained nearly flat. Gregg thought she was very business-like but also appeared genuinely concerned that they all understood her basic concepts. As she was concluding her remarks, he sensed a gentle tug on his trouser leg. Looking down he noticed a yellow Post-It note on the floor. In his own handwriting he read, "Define the business!" *I didn't write this. How in the world...? Okay, thanks, Mac.*

Standing up, Gregg reached into his briefcase and tossed each person a miniature football, which he'd picked up on the way home from work the day before.

"I'd like each of us to describe the pure basics of Herbert and Associates. What is our football?" Gregg asked.

"I guess it's the game we're playing," Mike answered, tossing the football up in the air and catching it again.

"Right. And what is the game we are playing?"

"We are sales reps for the Southeast," replied Mike.

"George, if I gave you that definition would you be able to describe Herbert and Associates?" questioned Gregg.

"I'd know we are a distributor in a geographic area, but that's about it." George paused. "There's got to be hundreds of distributors in the same area, so that really doesn't say much about us."

"Exactly. So how do we begin to define our business? Who are we? What do we do?"

Sally spoke up. "If you look at the sales breakdown you could say we are reps for small industrial equipment, tools and allied sundry items." Turning the page in her notebook she continued, "The breakdown shows we have averaged seventy-one percent of our sales in industrial equipment, twenty-three percent in pneumatic tools, and six percent in sundries."

"Great, so let's get rid of the tools and sundries and concentrate on the industrial equipment!" shouted Mike.

Sally was about to speak when Gregg cut her off. "What other information do you need to make that decision, Mike?"

"Nothing. It's all there. Sally just told us we did most of our business with industrial equipment."

Glancing towards Sally, Gregg pleaded, "Help us out. What other information should we know so as not to make a rash conclusion?"

Instead of answering him, Sally turned to Mike. "Mike, you are thinking the same way you were when I met you ten years ago. Look at sales! Who is the accountable person for sales?" she asked, her voice rising.

"Time out!" Gregg bellowed, a little more loudly than he intended. Holding his hands in the shape of a T, he proceeded in a calmer tone. "We came here today to improve our business, and that has to start with our thinking. The company is not what we think it is; it is what the customers perceive it to be. To define the business we have to understand the market, how we can satisfy the needs of the market, and what actions are needed to become profitable." He added, "In the past we've only been dealing with the symptoms of our business. We must discover our issues so we can make the right decisions. We have to first be sure we are asking the right questions."

"Good for you, Gregg. I don't know who's been whispering in your ear, but please keep listening," Sally said, smiling.

She flipped to the next PowerPoint slide. "Take a look at the profit report. Of the three categories of merchandise we carry, sundries produce a gross profit of forty-five percent, by far the highest of the three. Pneumatic tools generate thirty-three percent, and on its best day we might squeeze out twenty-six percent on industrial equipment," Sally explained to confused faces. "The average sale in dollars for industrial equipment is $12,500, and for tools it drops to $4,500. Even on the high side, sundries' average sale invoice is $1,100."

George cleared his throat. "I've never tried to put a cost on fulfilling these three categories, but common sense would tell me it costs more in labor to pull the sundry items than a tool or even a pallet jack or rolling cart."

"And if you look at the number of lines on an invoice," added Sally, "it takes more time to handle the paperwork for sundries than the invoices for industrial equipment or tools."

"So it takes us more time to pull, pack and ship the sundries. The tools come from the manufacturer's in shipping containers and the industrial equipment is already crated," voiced George.

"The point is," Sally continued, "we have to determine what our lines should be based on customer demand, not on our likes and dislikes. We must change. Change where needed will help us improve our growth and profits."

Gregg was struck with sudden inspiration. "Would you want to be treated by a physician using medical techniques and drugs that are five or ten years out of date?" he asked looking into the eyes of his staff.

"Well, neither would I. We have to ask ourselves, what is our company and what should it be? And in terms of today's business climate, not the way we remembered it to be. What is taking place in the market that we are not aware of? Are our customers going to our competition because we are not providing the goods and services they're demanding?"

George gave Mike a look that could kill. "Well, Mike, you're in the field with our customers all the time. What do you think?"

Mike appeared at a loss for words. Gregg didn't know if he should feel sorry for him or agree with George. It didn't matter. What concerned him the most was finding the answers. But what were the questions? Were they asking the right ones?

Mike was trying to put the pieces together. "If I listen to you, which is a novel concept for me I must admit, I can visualize the time required to pitch a pneumatic tool. It has to be demonstrated, and often it's awkward for the rep to set up the demo. Seldom is a sale completed at the time of the demonstration, and if there is any interest it takes a follow up visit to explain the details of the tool, its applications, warranty and so forth. In a way, the equipment is pretty basic and orders or reorders are simple to take. Most of the sundry orders are sent in on the Internet and the rep spends little time dealing with them. So what does all this mean?"

Remembering one of the comments he'd heard during his trip with Mac, Gregg asked, "Mike, why do you refer to selling a tool that averages over four thousand dollars as pitching a product?"

"Because that's what it is!" retorted Mike.

"Sorta sounds like a used car salesman in a plaid suit with a stained tie in need of a shave to me," observed George.

Gregg spoke hastily, seeing indignation on Mike's face. "We not only have to examine the figures, but we also have to take a hard look at our philosophies, especially in dealing with our customers. If we want to be professional we have to act the part and fill that role. I believe our philosophies for treating our customers are as basic as the footballs in front of you. But for now, let's stay with the numbers. We will come back to these other thoughts after lunch."

Sally continued with her explanations. After quite a few dumbfounded looks from her colleagues, she stopped and turned to Gregg. "I think for the first time I am beginning to understand the practical difference between defining blocking and tackling, and defining the 'basic' football. What's common to me is not common to you three. I guess I've been asking too much of you guys by expecting you to already know debits and credits."

As the meeting continued, it appeared to Gregg that Sally had lost the edge in her voice and was taking over the role of not just accountant, but teacher. Her examples were easier to understand as her patience grew with each exchange. Gregg was also encouraged by the questions Mike and George had been asking. Many of them were the same as his own. He hated losing Sally and wished Mickey Mouse ticking away on his desk could magically change her mind.

With thirty minutes left in the meeting, Gregg turned the conversation to defining the business. "Let's talk about who we are and who our customers are. It doesn't have a great deal of meaning to only use our three categories to define us. Mike, what do you think our customers are saying about our company?"

Mike hesitated. "Gregg, I'm ashamed to tell you I just do not know. When I meet with the reps, we chitchat, tell a few jokes, and occasionally go out for a meal," he confessed. "I might help with a demo and answer a technical question here and there, but we never seem to get around to discussing each other's business."

Gregg thought for a moment. "Mike, I want you to take some time to find out our customers' perception of us." As he was about to change direction of the conversation another Post-It note "appeared" among his accounting material: "Time for an action plan."

Gregg got up from his seat and pulled the flip chart easel over for all to see, wondering where to begin. Suddenly he felt a force in his fingers, and they began to write on the pad. This phenomenon reminded him of watching the keys depress on the keyboard of a player piano.

"Instead of moving on to the next topic as we so often do, I want all of us to go through a new process that was introduced to me recently. It's called an action plan; it's not complicated, but it is very thorough, and it will help you figure out how to do what I've asked, Mike."

As Gregg's fingers moved across the board seemingly out of his control, the others watched, intrigued.

ACTION PLAN:				
WHAT	HOW	WHO	WHEN	STATUS

He explained the What, How, Who, and When. "Take a look how the format develops as we go back to what I asked Mike. I've been aware of myself walking out of an office, yelling over my shoulder for something to take place. I wasn't clear with my directions, and I set no expectations or deadlines. That, too, will stop."

He looked around the room. His employees looked impressed and slightly taken aback. He asked, "Mike, what did it mean to you when I asked you to determine our customers' perception of Herbert and Associates?"

"Not much," Mike answered truthfully. "I thought I would figure it out the next time I met with a customer."

"And when would that be?" asked Gregg.

"Probably sometimes next month when I started my quarterly tour with the reps."

"I appreciate your honesty, Mike. This is a wonderful opportunity to close the awareness gap by my not assuming you will or will not do what I have envisioned in my brain. You aren't a mind reader, are you?" Gregg asked, and the others laughed.

"Mike, I want to make sure you understand what I mean by 'customers' perceptions' in all of its aspects. Start with describing how you would undertake the action plan," Gregg instructed.

Mike thought for a moment. "Well, I need to talk with a few customers and determine how they see us. I guess what they think about our pricing and our products, and maybe what they think about our reps."

Gregg was encouraged. "That's a start. Now help me with writing down a description of the plan at the top of this chart."

After several minutes of back and forth conversation, Gregg wrote on the first line of the chart what the two had agreed upon:

ACTION PLAN: *Determine our customers' perception of Herbert and Associates.*

"Now, what are the actions that have to be taken to determine this perception?" asked Gregg. As Mike answered Gregg began to write in the What column.

ACTION PLAN: Determine our customers' perception of Herbert and Associates				
WHAT	HOW	WHO	WHEN	STATUS
Determine what the customer thinks about our products.				
Determine what the customer thinks about our pricing				
Determine what the customer thinks about our delivery service.				
Determine what the customer thinks about our warrantee and return policies.				
Determine what kind of business they think we are in.				
Determine how they view our reps and their professionalism				
Determine how they would grade us overall.				

"You know, Gregg, this is going to make my life a great deal easier," announced Mike. Staring at the pad he continued, "I would have gone to the market with very little pre-thought, and I am absolutely sure I would not have covered more than one or two of these actions. Going through this process, I can begin to see your thinking, and it's helpful. I can't wait to fill in the next columns!" He was sitting forward on the edge of his chair.

"Okay, then, how are we going to determine what the customers think of our products?" Gregg asked.

As Mike and Gregg discussed the expectations the How column began to take shape.

ACTION PLAN: Determine our customers' perception of Herbert and Associates				
WHAT	**HOW**	**WHO**	**WHEN**	**STATUS**
Determine what the customer thinks about our products.	➢ Develop a list of customers according to their volume they with the company ➢ Divide that list by each category carried by the customer ➢ Meet with the decision makers who made the decision to carry that category.			
Determine what the customer thinks about our pricing, delivery service, warrantee and return policies, Determine how they would grade us overall. Determine how we could be a better supplier.				

"We're off to a great start," Gregg commented to the group. He was gratified to see George and Sally taking notes, and went on. "Who is accountable for each of the items in the Who column?"

"Sally and I will put the list together; we will be accountable," responded Mike.

"Oh, no," interjected Sally. "There can only be one person accountable, and that is you. I'll help, but the burden rests on your shoulders," she quipped.

"Okay, Gregg, make me the accountable person and add Sally's name."

Gregg highlighted Mike's name and wrote Sally's underneath. Then they all agreed on a time that met Gregg's expectations, and the first action with the first expectation was complete in all columns.

ACTION PLAN: Determine our customers' perception of Herbert and Associates				
WHAT	**HOW**	**WHO**	**WHEN**	**STATUS**
Determine what the customer thinks about our products.	➢ Develop a list of customers according to their volume with the company	**Mike** Susan	By 3:00 PM 10-12	
	➢ Divide that list by each category carried by the customer	**Mike** Susan	By 3:00 PM 10-14	
	➢ Meet with the decision makers who determine to carry that category.	**Mike** Reps	Begin within one week 10-21 and complete prior to 11-15	
Determine what the customer thinks about our pricing, delivery service, warrantee and return policies,	➢ Develop a survey for collecting and tabulating information	**Mike** Reps Susan	Begin within one week 10-21	
	➢ Meet at least five customers in each volume range per category	**Mike** Susan	Begin within one week 10-21 and complete prior to 11-15	
Determine how they would grade us overall.	➢ Ask how they would rate us compared to our competition	**Mike** Rep	Begin within one week 10-21 and complete prior to 11-15	
	➢ Based on collected information create a ranking	**Mike** Susan	Prior to 12-1	
Determine how we could be a better supplier.	➢ At the end of the survey ask what other ways could we improve	**Mike** Rep	Begin within one week 10-21 and complete prior to 11-15	
Meet with executive staff to discuss	➢ Review information and determine necessary action to be taken	**Mike** Susan George Gregg	9:00 AM 12-3	

The group spent the next ten minutes on the action plan, pleased with their success.

"I want to know why we haven't been doing this before," Mike said when they were finished. "It all appears to be so logical."

Looking down at his hands, Gregg answered, "Mike, I believe we were not ready for this step. But we are now, and we need to make the most of it." All nodded their heads in agreement and reviewed the now completed action plan. After a few more fine points were covered and several questions answered regarding the timing of certain events, Mike spoke up again.

"I'm excited about this new concept but equally frustrated with how I have been filling my role. You know, I feel as if I have headed up the sales function in name only. I haven't been managing anything. Yeah, I've put out a lot of fires and probably became more adept, but sales has not been a proactive function of the business."

"Ditto that for me, too," added George.

Thinking the same applied to him, Gregg said, "I heard a great quote not long ago. 'Yesterday is history, tomorrow is a mystery, and today is the present.' The presenter explained that the present has two meanings: it is both the current time and it is a gift. If we dwell too much on the past we will have a tendency to rely on it, and the future is built on the past and the present. From now on," he emphasized, "let's all work in the present and consider it the gift we can give others by making the future a better place to live and work."

He looked at his watch. "Our time is running out for today. For our staff meeting tomorrow morning, I want you, Mike, to begin reporting on your action plan. Sally, based on today's information, plan a training session for improving our accounting knowledge of the company, and I'll put some thought into the philosophies and values of the business. I want us to begin working on our mission, vision, and statement of beliefs. But remember, the sales numbers don't tell the whole story. Our customers vote with their dollars, so we have to know *why* they are willing to spend them on purchases from us."

Again Mike and George walked out ahead of Sally and Gregg. "I'm really impressed with today's meeting," voiced Sally to her boss. "I believe you're onto something, and you should see exciting results. I sorta wish I could be around to see the outcome."

Chapter 13

"Damn," slipped almost inaudibly out of Gregg's lips as he completely missed the overhead slam hit to his side of the court. "Liz, you are brutal!" he called across the net. "You have no mercy on a poor soul like me."

"Game, set, match," announced Bill as he and Liz gleefully ran to the center of the court to accept the Herberts' congratulations. Bill and Liz Knight had been playing mixed doubles with Gregg and Elaine since college, and the couples were best friends.

"That's another five dollars you owe us, and I will not take a check," Bill informed them good-naturedly.

"How about I buy lunch for you two and we call it even?" returned Gregg.

They walked to The Grill Room at the club for lunch. After their salads were served Bill observed, "Gregg, you seem like a changed man. I've noticed it for the past several weeks. You seem more relaxed and, well, at ease."

Liz added, "Bill's right. The last time we played and I hit the same overhead, your language would have embarrassed a sailor when you missed the return."

Neither Gregg nor Elaine responded. They just looked at each other and smiled.

"Oh no!" exclaimed Liz, her imagination on overdrive. "Don't tell me you're pregnant!"

"You're absolutely too quick to jump to conclusions," cooed Elaine. Leaning over the table she whispered, "But I do have a new lover."

Liz's eyebrows arched while Bill gave his familiar puzzled stare. Elaine and Gregg loved to tease their friends, who were far more serious by nature. Liz was a top researcher with a major pharmaceutical company while Bill headed up the biology department at the local university.

Liz asked, leaning forward, "Are you aware of this, Gregg?" With that, the other three exploded in laughter, loudly enough to catch the attention of the others eating lunch in the grill.

"Shhh," Elaine pleaded. "I don't want the whole world to know." After a purposeful silence she continued, "Gregg is my new lover. It's like we've fallen in love all over again."

Bill continued to look quizzically at Gregg while Liz inched closer for more details. "Don't stop now!"

Elaine obliged her. "You are both correct in your observations of Gregg. He's more lighthearted and he spends more time with his family. Didn't you notice that he actually showed up for tennis today? How many times have you called to play and I had to say no because Gregg was the office?"

"No more Saturdays at the office for me," Gregg announced. "At least not on a regular basis. I am trying to reorganize the business and prioritize my time. Bill, I know you're going to find this hard to believe, but I'm delegating more as you have suggested for years. I'm finally getting the concept of understanding and explaining expectations. I never understood why you took the extra time with the professors in your department; I thought you were micromanaging or babysitting, but now I realize that by taking a few more minutes up front you have saved countless hours. I've heard of your reputation around the university— how you're a wonderful professor plus an excellent administrator: a 'unique combination' was the exact quote.

"And besides increasing productivity I'm having less stress and beginning to experience that work can truly be fun."

Bill shook his head in disbelief. "That's really amazing, Gregg. What exactly has changed?"

Gregg pondered a moment. "Well, my staff had no idea of what was expected of them. In fact, I don't believe anyone in the company had an inkling. I'm sure this impacted our profits and the problems kept falling into my lap. I felt as if I was shouldering the whole load.

"More recently, the staff and I have been meeting to develop a mission and vision statement supported by our principles and beliefs. A customer survey is underway, and we plan to put all the information together to develop our game plan."

"What's a game plan? Why do you need one in business? I thought that was only for sports," interjected Liz.

"Liz, if I said I'll grab a bag of balls and let's hit some, what would you do?"

"I'd meet you on the tennis court and hit with you," she responded.

"But what if I had in mind hitting golf balls, and I went to the practice range instead? Then what?"

"I'd be improving my tennis and you would probably be ready to throw your golf clubs in the trash."

Gregg snapped his fingers. "That miscommunication was exactly what was taking place at Herbert and Associates. We were all playing a different game with different rules and outcomes. So the first thing we had to do was to realize what game we were in and the rules of play. Some of the staff thought we were merely reps going around taking orders; others believed we were marketing select categories of merchandise only to the businesses we were serving; a few thought we should grow outside our territory by adding new lines. Most thought the purpose of our business was to make a profit, but our associates didn't understand that profit is a yardstick that measures our efforts."

"Sounds like you were all going in different directions," Bill offered.

"You're right. And because of our lack of focus we were dealing with one crisis after another, putting out one fire while another started somewhere else. It was driving me up the wall. To make matters worse I kept trying to do what I had always done—work harder, not smarter. That's why I was rarely able to play tennis. I accepted all the responsibilities, and in my mind I was the only person accountable for the success or failure of the company. I'm sure I was the only one waking up at three in the morning in a near panic."

Bill shook his head. "Gregg, I had no idea."

Before his friend could say any more Gregg continued, "Don't feel sorry for me. I don't want you to go there. I'm telling you these things because you're my friend. I appreciate your support. But the real reason I am telling you all this is as a warning for you and Liz: improve your tennis game because I have to win back lots of five-dollar bets," Gregg warned Bill

The three of them shared a laugh as their meals arrived.

"Seriously Gregg, I am amazed. Tell me more about this new direction you are taking," Bill requested, taking a bite.

"It starts with our developing a mission statement but now we don't have all the facts to draft a final one. We still have to analyze the customer surveys, review the financials and meet with our prime manufactures for their input. What I have in my mind is a mission statement that sounds something like this: Herbert and Associates is a manufacturing representative of industrial equipment, pneumatic tools, and related sundry products. We build relationships with our customers to provide the products and services to support their individual goals. We will develop relationships with our current manufacturers as well as new ones to source additional products and services to satisfy our current and new customers' needs."

"I don't know how you can improve on that," added Liz.

Elaine had been about to take a sip of her iced tea, but she suddenly put the glass back down and said, "Tell them about the vision!"

Gregg grinned at her. "That, too, is in the working stage. But for now the vision might be: Herbert and Associates will become and remain the number one provider of our current products in our markets. We will measure this position by the increase in our customer base, product offerings and profitability. New products and services will be added to new and additional markets, providing both meet our mission and statement of values."

"I'm impressed," Bill said thoughtfully. "Keep refining the direction and mission, but don't get lost in the details."

Driving home, Gregg said to Elaine, "I really felt like today I was not only getting what I learned from Mac but now I can explain it to someone else. It's almost comical to think back at how I used to manage the company—rather, how it managed me. Elaine, I keep thinking what Mac said about 'fixing lives,' and I hope and believe I'll be able to impact all those I touch in business." He let out a deep breath. "I sure wish I could 'fix' Sally's. She was so helpful at the sales meeting last Monday; you could tell she'd worked really hard to make the material easy to understand. It would be terrible if she left the company."

The meeting had gone better than Gregg could have hoped; each sales manager now had an action plan not only for his region but to lead meetings of their own with their regions' sales reps.

"What will you have to do next?" asked Elaine.

"It has to be maintaining the momentum. I've always said the road to hell is paved with good intentions. I need to keep focused on the direction we're determining and not fall victim to the monkey theory. I have to see that we properly develop all of our associates."

"You have all my support. I know you'll succeed," Elaine said, touching his cheek.

After a restful and energized weekend Gregg returned to work on Monday with a newfound confidence that he could change the direction of the company. He could hardly believe it had been two weeks since his "journey" with Mac.

He picked up his notes for the day's staff meeting. He was pleased that they were occurring weekly. An announcement had been e-mailed last Thursday as a reminder along with the criteria for the weekly meeting. His desk was neat and there were only two messages for him.

Gregg rose and headed for the conference room, wondering if he would be the first to arrive. It was a few minutes before nine, and Sally and George were seated discussing some financial information. Mike arrived at the same time as Gregg.

"Good morning, everyone," Gregg greeted them. "We have ninety minutes to complete this staff meeting, so let's begin by each one giving the bullet points for today's discussion."

Going around the table, he wrote the highlights on the white board. Then Sally, Mike, and George each discussed the importance of their bullet points, marking them in red, yellow, or green.

"Okay," Gregg said when they were finished. "Let's start with the ones indicated with a red star on our agenda. Mike, why don't you begin?"

Mike cleared his throat. "I'm really concerned with the comments we are receiving from the customers surveyed. In a nutshell, they are not good. I'd go so far to say they are awful.

"A typical response is that the only reason the customer bought from us was because we had the distribution rights for the products they needed. Also, apparently many times we didn't make the promised delivery dates, and here's one calling us the most unprofessional business they have encountered." Flipping to another survey Mike continued, "This one compares our rep to a clown."

Gregg had already decided not to react emotionally to these comments, which had been his previous style. Even so, his heart rate increased and he felt his chest burn. He took a couple of deep breaths.

"Mike, we definitely have some serious issues. I believe this is only the tip of the iceberg. This is going to take too long to discuss here. I would like you to check with Nancy and schedule a time when you and I can have conference calls with all the individual sales reps. We need to follow up on the conference from last week and discuss these new issues."

The staff meeting continued with issues that could be addressed during the ninety minutes. The other topics were either put on hold for next week's meeting or allotted a time for discussion and action during the week. Finally, a couple of strategic issues were added to the monthly meeting's agenda.

The gathering ended on time and Gregg headed with Sally back to her office. "There was one thing I didn't understand at the meeting. Why did Don tell me last week he could not increase our line of credit as he has before?"

In an impatient tone she answered, "Gregg, if you look at the debt to equity ratio…" and then she paused. Finally, Sally continued with a more appropriate explanation of what constituted debt as well as equity or net worth, and showed Gregg with illustrations how the additional line of credit would not be a prudent risk for the bank.

"I never knew that was how Don looked at these numbers," Gregg mused. "He's tried to tell me many times before, but I just didn't want to hear what he had to say. After what you've told me, though, I wouldn't extend the credit either. What do we need to do to be more credit worthy?"

Sally set out a strategy that seemed plausible. Now that he understood the significance, Gregg was eager and willing to turn the situation around. He thanked Sally for her patience and asked her to explain the predicament to Mike and George to make sure each understood.

That afternoon, Mike had scheduled an appointment to further discuss the survey and the customers' perception of the company.

Gregg began. "I am devastated with these results, and I'm sure there will be other comments we don't want to hear. We have to right the wrongs of the past so we can change the customers' perceptions. Mike, their perception of us is reality to them, and it's going to take some doing to turn this mess around."

Mike's response surprised him. "Gregg, I've been a total ass. I've been doing a little soul searching, and I am ashamed of myself. I've been with the company almost as long as you, initially as the first regional sales manager, and now as VP of Sales. I've had the titles but I haven't filled either role," he admitted.

"We're both to blame," Gregg said. "I'm as much fault as you— maybe more. I took you, the best salesperson I had, and made you a manager. Mike, I set you up for failure and at the same time lost my best producer. But we cannot live in the past. What we *can* do is take action today."

"Well, I've done that," said Mike. "All thirty-five sales reps and managers are available for a conference call tomorrow morning at nine a.m.!" Seeing the pleased surprise on Gregg's face, Mike crossed his heart. "We are going to make this company the best it can be." He paused. "No, Gregg. We are going to make this company the leader in our field and set the standards to measure the results. If we don't hit that plateau then you have my resignation."

Before Gregg could respond Mike was out the door. He watched his sales VP pass Nancy's desk and exchange brief smiles with her, and wondered if they could turn their words into results. As he stood up to walk to the warehouse, he caught a glimpse of himself in a mirror. Noticing the small gold star on his lapel, he swore he would not only keep it but also earn Mac's trust for giving it to him.

Chapter 14

Gregg felt as if his new life was a roller coaster ride with exhilarating peaks and dreadful valleys. He remembered Mac telling him that life was not a series of ups and downs but rather resembled a railroad track, with one rail representing the good and the other the bad that we must deal with each day. Mac had added, "We have a tendency to only focus on one rail or the other without realizing we travel both the good and bad simultaneously."

Gregg could hardly believe the change in his company. Mike had taken initiative not only with the regional mangers but also with the sales reps themselves to create action plans for each one. Sally had been working tirelessly with him to help him understand the financials, and now Mike could see trends developing in the columns on the worksheets and was becoming familiar with the profit and loss statement, as well as the balance sheet. Next on his "financial to do" list was to understand the cash flow statement.

Just now, George had called to remind him of their meeting in the warehouse for the proposed forklift demo, and in his agenda Nancy had left him a note that he needed to take along the brochures and materials he'd received from the forklift vendor.

The meeting was scheduled in forty-five minutes, but Gregg wanted to go earlier to reacquaint himself with the present equipment and whether there were any issues with the forklift drivers. He arrived at the loading docks as the shifts were changing. Ever since hanging the mirror in his office, Gregg had become not only more aware of himself but also more observant of his surroundings. It seemed that learning to see himself more accurately also enabled him to notice other people and activities in a different light. He watched the workers gathering around the time clock waiting for the top of the hour so they could clock in and out.

Thinking back to his visit with Drew, Mac had explained how too many employees were "clock watchers" and never reached a higher level. They were there to put in a day's work for a day's pay. The challenge was to find ways for the hourly employees to become involved in the business as well and to make positive contributions. If an employee spent forty plus hours a week at work, then the work environment was one major key to his or her success—a fact that Gregg had given little attention to in the past.

Looking around the warehouse, he recognized the lead driver for the second shift. "Hi, Willie. How's the family?" he asked.

Willie was caught completely off guard. His puzzled look clearly said, *What's gotten into him?*

"We're all fine, Mr. Herbert," he answered.

"I've thought a lot about spending more time in the warehouse and talking with the guys." Before he could continue, Gregg caught the suspicion in Willie's eyes. "Willie," he said carefully, "it's not anything other than that I have been spending too much time in my office. I really don't know what is going on in my own company. If I don't see what's happening, I'm in no position to make things better or improve a particular situation."

The driver stood almost at attention waiting for Gregg to continue.

"How long have you been here?" Gregg inquired.

"Well, let's see, I'm going on my fourth year. Come here right out of the army."

"What did you do in the military?"

"I was a sergeant in the Transportation Corps," Willie replied. Pausing as if trying to figure out what to say next, he continued, "I'm going to East Carolina Technical School while working here nights." Then he relaxed a bit, adding, "Got a kid coming in two months."

"What do you want to do when you finish school?"

"I'd like to stay here, but I can't afford to with my wife quitting her job to have the kid."

It occurred to Gregg he would have never known any of this if he had not taken the initiative to engage Willie in this conversation. He couldn't even remember the man's last name. He vaguely remembered George remarking on what a good driver Willie was and how he seemed to take charge of the others, who liked him and looked up to him because he was older.

"I'd like to ask you a question," Gregg ventured. "Do you think most of the associates here care about their jobs?"

Willie sensed Gregg's concern and responded, "Some do; some don't."

"I want to be here to help you and the others earn more responsibility and dollars with the company. I need you to help me understand what's going on from their point of view."

Willie seemed torn. Finally, he said, "Mr. Herbert, the guys are pretty much up front with me and I do what I can to help them, especially the younger ones. I remember at their age I had no direction, I just came to work and waited for the weekends. A job at that time was only for a salary to pay the rent and grab a beer. I try to tell them not to waste their lives and to learn a vocation or skill. I know they don't want to spend the rest of their lives driving forklifts."

"What do you think the growth opportunities are with Herbert and Associates?" Gregg probed.

"Since you're asking, I'd say if you fit the mold you can move up; otherwise, look for another job."

"Why do you stay?" Gregg inquired.

"The company is close to my home and the school. We only have one car so it works for me."

"Have you ever considered moving up in the organization?"

"Not really," Willie answered, sounding as if he were thinking about something else.

Taking a chance Gregg stated, "You don't fit the mold."

"You got it," concluded Willie.

They started walking towards a driver maneuvering his forklift. "Look's like he knows what he is doing," Gregg observed.

"That's Squeaky. His real name is Ernest, goes to Tech with me. He was a corporal in my company and was discharged shortly after my tour of duty was over. We stayed in touch and he called one day saying he needed a part-time job while he was going to school. I mentioned Squ—Ernest to George, and he hired him about three years ago. He also works part time as a dispatcher with a local delivery company. He's trying to save enough money to start a family."

More information I didn't have, Gregg realized. *How could I have someone working here for three or four years and know practically nothing about him?*

Continuing their tour of the warehouse, the two men watched several warehousemen stocking merchandise. Gregg asked, "Do you think those fellows come to work, punch the clock and leave?"

"I'm not sure I'm following you," Willie replied.

Leaning against a column, Gregg mentally rephrased his question. "Willie, do they come to work punch a clock or do they come in with a purpose?"

Willie thought for a moment. "Mr. Herbert, do you mean do they have a purpose being here? From what I've seen, the answer is the majority only goes through the motions. They watch the clock to see when it's time for lunch, take a break or to leave."

Clock watchers, Gregg confirmed to himself. *Spending forty or more hours at work with no purpose and certainly no direction or career development must be disheartening. If they aren't encouraged by the company, why should any employee care? They come in willing to work when they first join, get lost in the mediocrity of the environment, and leave. No wonder our turnover is so high. What a way to treat our most valuable resource.*

Gregg thanked Willie for his time and said he would be back to continue their dialogue soon. He could almost hear Willie thinking to himself, *Where have I heard that before?* He was clearly not expecting to talk to Gregg again.

After the forklift demonstration Gregg headed to the HR department where Kristin was busy at her desk. She looked startled to see him. "Oh, Gregg, I didn't hear you come in. What can I do for you?"

"There are two forklift drivers working second shift. I only know their first names, Willie and Ernest. May I see their personnel folders?"

Gregg could tell from her response that the HR Director didn't know who they were, either. Looking through the company roster, she finally located the two files and handed them to Gregg.

He took the files and thanked her. *Focus on the railroad tracks; one is the good part of life, the other is the bad. All is not bad there's got to be some good taking place somewhere*, he said to himself, hoping it to be true.

He wanted so much for his employees to share his newly discovered passion for the company. Somehow he had to find a way to make them feel they were truly a part of what was going on with Herbert and Associates. His management team seemed to be getting it, although Mike was notoriously impetuous and often ran out of steam on new projects. It was Sally, however, that most worried and frustrated Gregg. She had been working hard to help them change, but she was still determined to leave.

When he got back to his office, he called Earl Wallace's cell phone and asked if his old friend could meet for Saturday breakfast. Earl had given Gregg his first black eye in the second grade. Gregg had lost contact with his childhood friend when Earl left for West Point and a brief career in the army. After fulfilling his military obligations, Earl entered the corporate world as an assistant director of personnel for a Fortune 500 company. He had worked his way up the corporate ladder and attended school at night to earn a masters degree and then a PhD. Tiring of travel, he opened a HR Consulting Firm, which developed a statewide reputation. When Earl returned to his hometown, his friendship with Gregg rekindled and they now met for breakfast several times a month.

Earl was always early for any appointment, even on the weekends, and had already arrived at the Marina Café, and was reading the paper, when Gregg walked in the next morning.

Gregg tossed out his usual greeting. "Doctor Wallace, I presume."

They ordered breakfast and caught up briefly. As they were on their second cups of coffee, Earl asked,

"So what's this emergency meeting about?"

Gregg stated, "I think I need some help with the HR piece of my business."

Quick-witted as well as to the point Earl stated, "Think you need help, or know?"

"I definitely need to talk to you about my company, especially how we treat our employees. I need you to look at our compliance issues. I also want to improve how we identify and develop those with the most potential."

He went on to explain his encounter with Willie and what bothered him when meeting with Kristin. "She didn't know the two forklift drivers' full names when I was inquiring about their personnel files. Earl, we aren't so big that the director of HR shouldn't be familiar with the names of each individual associate. I'm beginning to recognize that we aren't treating our most valuable resource like we should. I suspect we're doing only the mere requirements to get by. I asked Kristin about turnover and she said she'd have to run some reports; from her comment I'm pretty sure she has no idea about the magnitude of the issue."

Earl nodded in understanding. "I think it's been at least five years since you had me conduct an employee survey."

Gregg clarified, "We haven't had any major complaints from our employees, and I took that to mean everything was okay. Something tells me we need to find out more."

"I call what you are talking about as an 'employee audit,'" Earl responded. "It gives management indications of personnel issues before they become problems. In all my experiences, I typically find employee issues are not acute; rather, they are chronic and simmer over different periods and lengths of time. Too often management has on blinders and fails to see a trend before it's too late."

Gregg jumped back in. "Now that you mention it, over the years I've observed what you're talking about. I know I must be guilty of not paying close enough attention to the human side of our business. If a personnel problem was dropped into my lap, I handed it off in such a manner I am sure I was perceived as getting rid of a hot potato." He shook his head in disbelief.

"I read an article in a recent trade journal," Earl said. "It was talking about how most employees don't know where they fit into the total picture of the work area. If they don't know what they can do to improve the business, then they have no passion for their jobs and do the minimum to get by. On the other hand, if associates know and understand where their duties fit into the grand scheme of the company—like how they are contributing to sales or gross margins, or to reducing expenses or overhead—they're more motivated to maximize their full potential. Particularly if they understand that their contributions will be rewarded."

Gregg agreed with the article Earl was describing. "It seems my employees don't understand the purpose of their positions; I get the feeling that they're just clock watchers going through the motions."

Earl leaned forward. "Gregg, you hit the nail on the head. But in some organizations, management believes that only the supervisory level and above have a need to truly understand their jobs. It should be of no concern to the hourly worker; some bosses even think they wouldn't understand if you told them."

"That doesn't sound very smart to me when I hear you say the words, but I'm not even sure the supervisors truly understood how they should do their jobs," Gregg lamented.

Earl gave an understanding chuckle. "Typically most of the companies I work with have some variation of a business plan and budget. In the more successful organizations both the plan and budget are well thought out and communicated throughout the organization."

"You mean all the way down to the hourly people?"

"Yes, especially the hourly people."

Gregg felt momentarily overwhelmed. "If my staff doesn't understand the concepts behind planning and budgeting for my company, how in the world will the hourly employees? I mean, how do you explain a strategic plan and a financial budget to an hourly employee?"

"Oh, Gregg, you make things so complicated. Just explain the plan and budget in terms they understand and make the numbers and goals meaningful to each individual."

"That's it?" Gregg couldn't keep the disbelief out of his voice.

"Business isn't hard. It's the people within the business that make it complicated. My theory is that employees will live up to the expectations of their bosses. You need to raise your expectations of the employees throughout your company."

Earl paused thoughtfully. "I have an intern who is working on his masters degree. He's had five or six years of experience, and a quick look-see into your company would be right up his alley. Based on what he finds we can decide what actions to take."

"Earl that would be fantastic."

"Education has to take place at all levels within a company," Earl said. "The more your employees understand the goals and how they can make a meaningful contribution, the more successful they will be, as well as the company.

"One of my most successful clients is a distributor similar to you. The two of you began about the same time, and now their revenues exceed fifty million dollars. They are extremely profitable, they develop their supervisors and managers from the existing personnel, and they have little turnover of employees." He raised his eyebrows. "Your counterpart is currently on an extensive trip to Europe studying the migration patterns of some kind of waterfowl. He can take off on trips because he knows he has developed a highly motivated and productive organization—from top to bottom."

Gregg felt himself sinking into the café booth. "All right. What's your intern's name?"

"Mark Burbage. I'll have him contact you on Monday," replied Earl.

He picked up the check and rose to walk to the cashier stand. "Come on, Gregg, it really isn't hard. We'll talk some more about that later. Say hello to Elaine and the kids."

With that exchange Earl was out the door, and Gregg watched as he tucked his tall, lanky frame into his new BMW two-seater.

Gregg stood in the parking lot looking out over the harbor. *I started out with a passion for beginning the business, but somewhere along the way I lost it. Now it's resurfaced, thanks to Mac. I've rekindled my passion, and I have to figure out a way to ignite the passion of every employee. Why would I want to come to work each day to just get paid? Why would I want to stay with any company that did not facilitate my development and growth? It would be absolutely frustrating doing the same thing over and over again, only to receive a paycheck with no understanding how I could advance. I would just be stuck in a dead end job. How exciting could that be?*

Chapter 15

The following week Mark Burbage completed the employee audit and analyzed the information he had gathered. After Earl reviewed the results, he called Gregg.

"It's Dr. Wallace for you," Nancy informed Gregg.

"Hello. How's the doctor?" Gregg greeted his friend.

"Not bad, but I would be a whole lot better if I could improve my tennis game. How about giving me a lesson soon?" Shifting back to the main topic, Earl continued, "I want to pick a time to review the findings of the employee audit and show you a PowerPoint presentation."

Checking calendars, the two made an appointment for Friday at eleven a.m. "I'll come over to Herbert and Associates and then you can buy me lunch."

"Better still," Gregg suggested, "how about after we meet we go to the club for lunch and volley some balls afterwards?"

"You're on. But take it easy on me. See you Friday," Earl acknowledged.

On Friday Gregg ushered his friend into the conference room where a PowerPoint projector had been set up.

Earl got right to the point. "Gregg, Mark's findings are not unusual for a company your size with similar management styles and culture. Besides the typical communication and morale issues, which we'll address later, I want to focus primarily on your management team. The expression making its way throughout the business community—"getting the right people on the bus and getting them into the right seats"—fits your company to a T. As Jim Collins explained in his book, *Good to Great*, if you're going to take a company in a specific direction and focus on a particular set of goals, you first have to have the team on board and in the correct positions. I'd be interested to learn how you picked your management team."

Gregg answered slowly. "I'm not sure if I picked them or if they just evolved. Some I knew prior to them joining the company; others were looking for work and I liked them. Earl, I don't know, the team just came together."

"And as the company grew, how did you select your executive team?" Earl asked.

"Mike was our best salesperson so I made him sales manager and then VP of Sales. George worked his way up through shipping and receiving then became a supervisor and later headed up the warehouse. Sally's aunt used to work for the company and that's how I met her. Did I tell you she's leaving?"

"No, but I'm not surprised. Let's take a look at Mark's rundown on Sally," Earl suggested, bringing out a piece of paper. Glancing over it, he said, "Sally is totally frustrated in her position. She really doesn't want to leave, but to use her words, she's fed up to her ears. She has mixed feelings; on one side she loves what she's doing and can see the potential of the company. On the other hand she believes it will take too long to make the changes all of you have been discussing, and by then she predicts you'll run out of cash.

"On a positive note," he added, "Sally acknowledged all the changes you and your team are currently making, and that you have come a long way in a short period of time."

"I'm very aware of the situation with Sally," Gregg said testily. "Let's move on and I'll deal with her at another time."

"All right." Earl hooked up his computer to the projector. "I want to go through the complete presentation and then answer your questions when I have finished. This will allow you to see the whole picture, and some of your questions may be answered during the slide show."

Gregg sat attentively as Earl went through the material and jotted down a few notes to discuss at the conclusion. When the presentation ended, he requested, "Go back to the slide where you discussed talent assessment."

Earl produced the slide.

	Individual may be promoted up to two levels	Individual may be promoted up one level	Individual has maxed at current level
A-Level This individual exceeds expectations	Individuals in light gray squares are ready to move up		Individuals in dark gray squares are at maximum level
B-Level This individual fully meets expectations		Individuals in white squares have a high potential	
C-Level This individual partially meets expectations			

"So what I should be looking for are the employees who are in the light gray squares and then those in the white," Gregg concluded. "But how do you start fitting the individuals into the squares?"

"The best way is to use the Position Development Plans you recently told me about for each of your associates," Earl said. "Although many of the people I've observed in the light gray squares are self-starters and well disciplined, they still require goals and development, and there must be ways of measuring their performance. Guessing or assuming how they've performed or putting them into the light gray because you like them is not reason enough."

He looked expectantly at Gregg, who said, "Well, the truth is we have nothing that comes close to resembling your diagram. Guess you better help us put one together."

"Companies that are top performers in their industry basically have top people in place and in the correct positions," Earl explained. "They're given the tools to be successful, and there is a high level of expectation of their performance. These individuals are typically selected early in their careers and are groomed and developed to become tomorrow's leaders. They fully understand their jobs and perform at a level that exceeds expectations.

"Gregg," he said, glancing over at his friend, "to reach these higher levels there have to be yardsticks in place to measure performance. And these yardsticks must be understood by both the individual and his or her immediate supervisor."

Gregg couldn't help but remember his discussion with Mac about yardsticks.

Earl continued, "From my experience and Mark's input concerning your associates, I agree with you that your leaders have evolved into place. They were not selected as the best available for the position.

There was no match up of their abilities with the requirements of the position, and if they were successful it was probably because of pure luck."

"But you said that none of your findings were unusual and that a great deal of these companies are in the same boat. Why do you think so many of us have let our personnel evolve, as you put it?" asked Gregg.

He cringed inwardly as Earl described the struggles of a small business owner trying to manage his or her business. Attempts to grow a company while micromanaging employees usually lead to failure. The company will not grow beyond the owner's ability to manage all aspects including effective delegation, much like Mac had explained. This in turn leads to sketchy management job descriptions resulting in an overall mediocrity in a management team that has no direction, no accountability, and little motivation.

"To add fuel to the fire," Earl concluded, "these managers have two mindsets. The first is one of good intentions to perform and believing that they can do their job. Sometimes they feel they are infallible and make unrealistic commitments. Then, when things go wrong, they move into the second mindset, which is denial.

"Gregg, I'm sure you've asked one of your managers to do a job and the result did not meet your expectations. Don't they give you many excuses blaming their unsuccessful outcome on someone or something else?"

"Earl, I hear you loud and clear, but it doesn't make sense!" Gregg responded sharply. "Why does this happen?"

"One main reason is that the managers have no ownership in the consequences," Earl answered, pausing for his words to sink in. "What happens when one of your managers or executives does not accomplish a goal or task?"

"I guess we talk about it and figure out what comes next," Gregg answered weakly.

"And if this kind of performance persists, what do you do?"

"I don't know. I guess it depends on how badly the job was done," Gregg thought out loud.

"Has anyone ever lost their job because of this kind of behavior?"

"Of course not!" Gregg answered. After a lull, he continued as if lost in another world, "Oh, I see where you're going with this reasoning. If there are no consequences for poor performance, I just continue to accept it—even reward it."

Earl nodded in agreement. "Now you can see that if there are no consequences, there can be no ownership. In other companies this performance is tolerated over the years. Then, when a major issue arises and the results are devastating for the company, it usually means that there's no other alternative but to terminate that manager. When this happens, the individual is mystified because he or she has been performing the same way for years. That's not a very effective way of developing and rewarding your management team."

"Guilty as charged," was Gregg's only reply.

Earl's tone was gentle. "It's not my purpose to cause you to feel guilty. I want to see you establish a program for developing and rewarding your associates, starting with your immediate staff. A program that outlines the development process, establishes rewards and defines consequences—and I don't mean only termination," he explained.

"What are other consequences that can be used that are effective in the development process?"

"If you have the Position Development Plans tied into the performance reviews, it makes your life as an executive less stressful in developing your managers. You're working with your staff on a defined basis to identify points for improving performance. And you also have a personal accountability in your direct reports' success. If an individual goes off course and you're a part of the development process, then you're able to catch it quickly and can make a small correction to put him or her back on track. If the poor behavior continues, the individual can receive counseling immediately. If this behavior doesn't improve, a verbal or written warning may be given. A next step in the correction process is for the associate not to earn a bonus or not to receive a salary increase.

"The key to remember, Gregg, is to deal with negative behavior quickly so necessary action can be taken directly following the inappropriate behavior. As I say, one or two 'slaps on the wrist' are not that painful and are typically all that's needed. When you're in touch with your subordinates through the PDPs, all of you know the performance standards and how each person is being measured against them on a predetermined timetable. Termination of a manager is more tied into their overall lack of development than a specific instance."

Gregg's immediate reaction had been that his long time friend was reprimanding him. But as Earl's explanations continued and the emotions dissipated, Gregg realized the truth behind his comments.

"All right. Let's look at the other slides that show the process for developing an associate," he suggested.

As he flipped to the next slide, Earl said, "An executive, manager or supervisor must know the people they're working with and be able to communicate with them on a deeper level. Most top managers don't know their peer group and have little or no interest in knowing their subordinates well enough to understand their motives, personal goals and passions."

"What does passion have to do with all of this?" asked Gregg, vaguely remembering Mac's insistence that work should be fun.

"I'll get to that in a minute. But for now look at this slide."

The slide posed four issues that the PDP should address:

1. Do you know your job?

2. Who have you developed?

3. Are you learning the job of the person above you and teaching the job of the person below you?

4. What is the amount of "quality time" that you have spent developing people in the organization?

"As a manager of an individual," Earl began, "you must know this person's abilities, attitude, and in particular what drives them to success. The answers to the four questions on the slide begin to give you insight into what the reporting person knows about his or her job and interest in developing others.

"As an example, suppose I'm a manager in your organization. If I want to be promoted, I cannot leave a vacancy behind; therefore, I must teach my job to the person who will fill it and begin learning the job I will be taking. A process must be established in order for this to take place within an organization.

"Too often leaders of a company don't know the person that will take their place, nor do they have a thorough understanding of the position needing to be filled. It's like trying to put a square peg in a round hole—it just doesn't fit, and the person selected is set up for failure not success. To avoid this, one concept to understand is that when promoting from within or selecting a new hire, a manager or executive should know the scope of the position, the duties required, and the expectations you have for that individual."

Earl changed the slide to show requirements for the PDP template.

✓ Scope of position

✓ Essential duties to earn salary or bonus wage

✓ Bonus performance criteria

✓ Obstacles, challenges, and identified areas of improvement

✓ Position Development Plan (PDP)

✓ Qualification requirements

"This is starting to get complicated," complained Gregg.

"Anything that's new and not immediately understood seems complicated," Earl admitted. "But if you take the time to learn the concepts, you'll reap the rewards later. When the owners, principals, and senior management of a company have a positive outlook and are determined to be the best they can be, the organization will adopt those same qualities. Gregg, it's *essential* to remember that a company takes on the personality and attitude of its top leaders."

Earl grabbed a bottle of water and continued, "When starting to match the associate to the position you also need to know the individual and the obstacles in their development, as you see on the next slide. Talking to someone as an adult results in the other person acting like an adult. So many times in my career I've watched a manager talking to a subordinate like a parent to a child. As a result, the 'parent' doesn't receive an adult response and so continues the same communication style. The 'child' responds in an immature manner, and we have a disconnect in the communication process. Ultimately, the manager decides that the subordinate and the position are not a match."

He changed the slide. "Instead both manager and subordinate have to look at the situation from a realistic point of view."

UNDERSTANDING THEIR REALITY

✓ Know the person before you sit down with them.

✓ When reviewing the obstacle sheet, be empathetic and "wear the other person's shoes."

✓ Communicate adult to adult, not adult to child.

✓ Determine where the other person is in reality, versus your assumptions about them.

"Gregg, this concept is all about being an effective leader. Take a look at what I consider to be the five steps to being such an individual." He changed the slide.

5 STEPS TO BEING AN EFFECTIVE LEADER

1. Hire and reward the best people.
2. Make sure your people know what the company's mission is— what is expected of them.
3. Make sure employees have the necessary resources to do their jobs.
4. Leave people alone to do their jobs; don't micromanage them.
5. Help your employees get unstuck; remove obstacles as they arise.

"Effective leaders hire the most qualified person they can find and afford for the position," Earl detailed, "not just a friend or the first so-called qualified person that comes through the door. Turnover is one of

the highest hidden costs in any organization. Reducing turnover begins with finding the right person for the right job, and giving them the proper tools and direction to be successful. When you have this combination, you don't have to micromanage; but you are there as a resource to remove any obstructions in the way of the individual's success. Their success is your success!"

Gregg held up his hands in a gesture of surrender. "Earl, this is all coming at me so fast. I need some time to absorb these concepts and practice applying them to my business. I do have a question for you, though. How do you manage an individual's growth and encourage better performance?"

"Good question." Earl projected the next slide on the screen and explained, "You have to look at a person's potential for personal growth. This means both for the individual as well as the company."

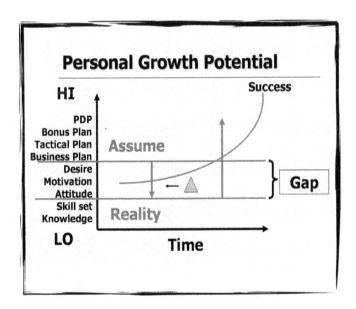

"Let's examine this concept from the point of view of the company. The organization is the framework for facilitating the growth of an individual. It must have in place a development plan like the PDPs, and these have to connect with the business plans of the company. An associate with Herbert and Associates must not only know the requirements of their position but also how they will be developed to be successful in their job. This creates a productive start. Knowing how an associate fits into the total scheme of the company and its plans helps them to feel they're making a contribution. The more they can contribute and be rewarded for their efforts, the more passion they'll have to be successful and support the success of the company."

He turned to his friend. "Gregg, you need to remember this basic concept: an individual's passion for coming to work and performing their job is directly related to the success they have in supporting the company in achieving its goals. The organization must provide the framework to support both the growth and development of the associate and the company.

"You probably know that you as the owner and principal must have passion first before you can expect your staff to have it. In the chain of command, everyone and everything should report to one member of your staff, and that member must be accountable for each area and each person reporting to him or her. If you remove the 'disconnects' that exist between the senior level of management and the remainder of the organization, this passion concept will filter down and later permeate the organization."

Pointing to the slide on the screen, Earl continued with his explanation. "The first four items illustrated are documents—only pieces of paper. The essence of success lies in desire, motivation, and attitude of the organization and its most important asset, its people—the living organism that brings the pieces of the business together."

As Earl took a sip of water, Gregg broke in with a question. "Why are the skill sets and knowledge at the bottom of the chart?"

"Think of it this way. The PDP and the business plans at the top are the documents needed to generate a direction for growth of the company and the individual. The middle three traits drive the individual and must be known both prior to and after hiring, especially by the immediate supervisor. The individual must have the skill sets and basic knowledge to do the job or they should not be hired. That's the job of the HR department and the manager or supervisor of the applicant or new hire."

"I haven't given this much consideration to the hiring process, and I'm sure none of the other managers have either. I haven't set a very good example for them," Gregg acknowledged. "You know, Earl, we may have hired people that weren't much more than warm bodies."

Sensing Gregg's remorse, Earl replied gently, "It's more important to recognize that a change needs to be made now than to worry about what transpired in the past. It takes commitment to make changes, especially after you've been in a routine for so long. If you have that resolve, I'll help you move forward." He slapped his hands to his thighs. "Now, come on, let's go eat and hit some tennis balls. You can help me with my serve. Boy, do I need to change my grip, my toss, my movement—"

"Okay, I get the message!" Gregg interrupted.

As they left the office, he felt almost as if he'd been on another journey with Mac. "I've talked about this long enough and it's time to take action, time to move forward," he muttered under his breath.

"What's that?" Earl asked.

"Oh nothing. Just trying to decide how hard to hit the returns," Gregg remarked as he ushered his friend out of the office.

It was good to have someone to share his dilemmas and frustrations with, he thought as they headed to the parking lot. *One day I'll be a worthy mentor and live Earl's examples. I'll fix lives as Mac does so well.*

On his desk, a notepad filled with writing lay open beside a stubby yellow pencil.

notes

✓ Every employee should understand the company's budget and business plan so they can know how they specifically contribute.

✓ Using the PDP, it's important to be aware of how the management team is performing against standards.

✓ Poor management should be met with immediate and appropriate consequences.

✓ Managers should relate to employees adult to adult, not adult to child.

✓ A company takes on the attitude of its top leaders.

✓ The organization is the framework for facilitating the growth of an individual.

✓ An individual's passion for coming to work and performing their job is directly related to the success they have in supporting the company in achieving its goals.

✓ Personal growth potential is a combination of concepts. PDP and business plans generate a direction for company and individual growth. Desire, motivation, and attitude drive the individual, who must also have the skill sets and basic knowledge to do the job.

Chapter 16

That night, Gregg woke up startled, sensing he was fighting his pillow. In his subconscious mind he had been fighting windmills but could not tell if he was winning or losing. He knew he wasn't having a panic attack, as he'd experienced from time to time. There was no interest payment due the next day, and there was more than enough cash to meet payroll. Then what was it? What had broken into his sound sleep?

I must be in information overload, he thought. Anyone would be tossing and turning after their head had been packed with tons of new data, first by Mac and then by the recent events he had experienced. Too much was happening, and it had only been a few months since his visit from Mac.

He slipped out of bed, careful not to wake Elaine. The full moon was lighting the window, so Gregg walked over to look out into the backyard. The patio and pool were quiet and the moon was reflecting off the water. As he turned away, he noticed a shadow of what appeared to be a person sitting on one of the lounge chairs. He pulled on a T-shirt and a pair of Docksiders, and tiptoed down the stairs to investigate.

It was a beautiful night and Gregg was momentarily distracted by the sounds of nature. He focused on the lounge chair and said to his surroundings, "I should have known it was you. Did you arrange for the moonlight to wake me, or was it the windmills you set up for me to battle?"

Mac turned in the lounge chair with a chuckle. "My spies tell me you're being exposed to many new and exciting ideas."

Gregg folded his arms across his chest. "New, yes, but I don't know about exciting, as they haven't all sunk in. I was thinking a few minutes ago that I was swimming in information overload. How are you, Mac? I've missed you."

Mac sat up, adjusted his chair, and patted the one next to him, indicating for Gregg to sit down. "I discovered a while ago that a second visit was appropriate about this time in order to offer some moral support in the development of one of my lambs. So tell me, Gregg, how are you doing?"

Gregg sat down and felt an instant relief at being next to his mentor. Sighing, he continued, "I can sum it up this way. I am energized, frustrated, challenged, overwhelmed, and confused. All these adjectives describe my state of mind. I hardly even know what to think when I look at myself in the mirror in my office."

"That's great," Mac responded with one of his knowing smiles.

Gregg was no longer taken aback by Mac or his unique, kindhearted behavior, even though sometimes he had no clue as to his meaning—like now. "Okay, wise old sage, tell me why all this is 'great.'"

Mac smiled. "You must be absorbing some of the 'information overload' or you wouldn't be having these feelings. I like your choice of words, especially your use of *challenged*. How do you explain your meaning of the word?"

Gregg crossed his ankles and slid down into a more comfortable position in his chair. "I'm challenged by the amount of information. I'm challenged by how to use what I am being exposed to, and I'm challenged to change my behavior, management style, and even my most intimate thoughts about myself. I also feel guilty—oh, I left that one out—about all the time I've wasted and where I could have been if I'd known years ago what I'm learning now."

"All normal feelings, my good man," confirmed Mac. "And you can rest assured that I've heard these and similar laments many times before. That's why I'm visiting you again.

"Here are a couple of thoughts that have proved useful to the other folks you met on our journey together. Think of all the information you are accumulating as what's needed to bake a cake. You have the very best flour, Grade A eggs, the finest chocolate—the purest ingredients to bake this cake. The receipt is a closely guarded secret from a famous French bakery and has stood the test of time." He paused, waiting.

"Now can I make the cake?" Gregg questioned, not knowing what he was supposed to say.

"Ah, now you have afforded me the opportunity I was looking for to alleviate some of your frustration and concerns," Mac said with a lilt. "Tell me, Gregg, just how do you plan to make this cake?"

"I've watched Elaine bake cakes hundreds of times. All you have to do is get out the cookbook and follow the recipe, measure the ingredients, slap it into the oven and wait for it to bake. Then take it out, ice it, and hurrah, it's time to eat," Gregg said sarcastically,

"Not so fast. I didn't commit my time to be with you and not be taken seriously," Mac reprimanded.

Gregg looked over at Mac and for the first time saw him frowning. "I'm sorry. I told you I was in information overload."

Mac sighed. "I wanted to make two points with the analogy I gave you. On some level, you can make things happen. But on another level, you have to *let* things happen. You can make the batter for the cake and put it in the oven. Then it's up to the oven to bake the cake, not you, and you have to allow the oven the time to bake it."

When he thought about it, Gregg realized he *was* trying to make everything happen. In fact, he was trying to make everything happen all at once. Recalling past events, he further realized that he was trying to make everything happen all at once and with no priorities. To be fair, this "concept of make things happen" versus "concept of let things happen" could not be nearly as challenging or frustrating as trying to make everything happen all at once, he reasoned.

With a small laugh, he said to Mac, "I think I'm beginning to recognize the significance of the windmills I've been jostling. But what I don't understand is how to let things happen. Aren't you supposed to be in charge of your own destiny? An owner, and all?"

Mac waved his hand to emphasize his answer. "Yes, and you are in charge. You became in charge as soon as you committed to making a change in how you manage your business and your life. But you keep forgetting that managing does not mean having to actually do things yourself. You manage The Process to accomplish your goals. You let The Process take over by creating expectations and accountability, and achieving closure on each action that is taken. When you manage The Process, you eliminate many of the personalities and emotions that get in the way. The action plans take away the micromanaging, enhances development, and creates focus."

Giving Gregg a measured look, Mac said, "Gregg, you are the leader of your company, not the supervisor. Supervisors work within the framework of the organization; leaders direct the organization to greatness. The captain of a ship is stationed at the helm. He doesn't handle the lines or repair the engines; rather, he plots and pilots the course. Sometimes I think you believe you have to be in the engine room with a wrench making sure the engines are performing properly. But if you're down there, who is at the helm?"

Good point, Gregg thought ruefully. "But I still don't understand how "to let things happen" at Herbert and Associates. How do I begin to use the information without feeling overloaded?"

"That's simple," Mac said with a smile. "Start using the Rule of Three.

By now Gregg had learned to be more patient with his mentor.

"I was driving to work a few days ago," Gregg said thoughtfully, "and I saw a message on a church signboard. It said, 'Happiness is a direction, not a place.' It made me think that I spend too much time concerning myself with the future outcome and not enough time in the present preparing to reach my goals. I need to take the knowledge you're sharing with me and the philosophy of Graham Williamson and mix the two."

"Graham Williamson?" For the first time Mac looked bemused. "I'm not sure I recognize the name. What's his area of expertise?"

With a genuine laugh Gregg answered, "He's my personal trainer, and his areas of expertise are flexibility, stability, power, and strength. Graham's young enough to be my son, but he has a wealth of knowledge of the body."

"And how are you planning to pair Mac the carpenter with Graham the trainer?" Mac asked with a grin.

Gregg felt as if the tables had been turned. It seemed he had an answer that was not in the carpenter's repertoire. "I started working out about ten years ago. I went three times a week to a fitness center with all the latest equipment. I felt I was working hard because I would be tired and sweaty afterwards. But part of the gym fee was an annual fitness assessment, and one year later at the end of my assessment I had made little or no improvement.

"I bumped into a friend at a cocktail party and at first didn't recognize him. He'd lost thirty pounds and looked great. He mentioned that Graham had helped him, so I called the trainer the next day. That was eight years ago. Sometimes I still have a battle with the scale, but I can keep up with the kids and have gotten rid of my middle budge and all those little aches and pains."

He laughed, remembering. "There were times I didn't want to meet him at five thirty in the morning. There were many times that I didn't want to do the last few reps, but he pushed me on and encouraged my efforts. I saw others come to work out without a coach, but after a few weeks or months they quit. It was especially interesting to watch those who worked with the exercise machines in January but were never seen again after March. Mac, I need a personal coach in business like I needed a personal trainer."

"I am your personal coach," Mac responded, spreading his hands wide in a gesture of generosity. "When you first started with Graham could you perform at the level you do today?"

"No, it took months to become accustomed to the program. And as soon as I came close to mastering a particular routine, Graham changed it and I felt like I was starting all over again. When I watched him balance on an exercise ball using only his knees, I thought there was no way I could duplicate that. Now I like to impress my out-of-shape friends by balancing on the ball and telling them it only took me a few tries when in reality it took weeks."

Mac laughed. "Well then. Don't expect to be a business body-builder right off the bat. Let's start your training regime with the Rule of Three. Make a list of what you need to accomplish to reach your personal and business goals. Place them in priority of importance as well as in chronological order. Then pick the top three and develop action plans for each one."

"Why three?" Gregg asked.

"One top priority isn't enough because you might not have all the data you need, or there may be others who should be in the plan with you but have scheduling conflicts. More than three is too hard to juggle, so stay with the Rule of Three. On your list, note the next priorities that should move up to the top when one of your top three is completed. This is a wonderful way to segment and prioritize your information overload without forgetting an important issue that needs to be handled at a later date. When you use this technique in your meetings to support the business plan and budget, you'll begin to see the Unity of Purpose we've discussed previously."

They spent another hour together until Gregg began to feel a calmness settle over him. Then he said, "Mac, I have to be at the office early. I want to prepare for our monthly strategy meeting. Sally will have the budget for next year. She's been working with Mike, George, and me to put it together. I have a draft of the business plan for next year, and now I'll introduce your Rule of Three to the group."

They said goodnight and Gregg headed back to his bedroom. He fell asleep immediately—so effortlessly; so peacefully.

***

Gregg could not help but notice that meetings were now starting promptly and those attending were well prepared. The company's atmosphere was changing from a lethargic and reactive to proactive and full of hope for the future. Sally had extended her stay another month, but he was not sure if this was permanent. Mike was becoming a true VP of Sales, and George was more involved than ever with the staff. He had also stopped belittling himself for not being as capable as the others.

"It's three months before the beginning of the new fiscal year and we're already looking at a business plan and a budget for next year," Sally announced to the group.

"We have all the information from our customer surveys, including the recaps from the focus groups. The input, although not what we wanted to hear, has been extremely helpful in developing a sales plan to support the overall plan of the company," informed Mike.

George entered the conversation without being invited. The lack of tensions in the room had encouraged his D and I behavior, prompting him to speak up more frequently. "We have streamlined the receiving and shipping process. Thanks to Willie and Ernest our new foremen, we're handling more inventory with less employees. They have made my life so much easier. I feel I'm finally in control of what's taking place in all areas of the warehouse."

Gregg stood up. "I'm proud of all of you and the effort you have given in supporting the company. You are setting great examples for each other as well as for all the employees, " he said. Words that would have been high praise from him and rarely spoken in the past were now becoming both commonplace and well deserved.

"But, boss, none of this would be taking place if you hadn't taken that little mysterious trip you've only hinted about," chimed in Mike with a wink.

"You're more on target than you realize," Gregg told him. "But let's move on with our agenda. We have lots to cover this morning. I'll start by reviewing the business plan. I see you each have a copy, and from the sticky notes I see attached I believe you have actually read it!"

The four had an excellent exchange of ideas and were able to fine-tune the document. The overall plan contained the supporting plans from sales, operations, and finance with clear expectations that tied all the planning ideas together. Then they turned to discussing the budget to quantify the business plan, Gregg leading the discussion to ensure the budget supported the value and principles, as well as fulfilling the vision and mission of the company.

"What concerns me," he said, "is that we all continue to be devoted to the success of our planning process and keep the momentum moving. The worst thing we can do to sabotage this process is not support it and each other. We have to all take ownership in our future. It's not my plan—in fact, it's not even your plan—it is Herbert and Associates' plan to obtain continued success for all of us. We can't just talk a good game; we have to actually play the game. And my personal hope is that we will develop a passion for what we are undertaking."

Gregg pulled out a copy of the final slide of The Process and distributed it the others. "Take a look at this handout, 'The Heart of the Matter.' It's a diagram of what we've been discussing, the key word at the top being *expectations.*"

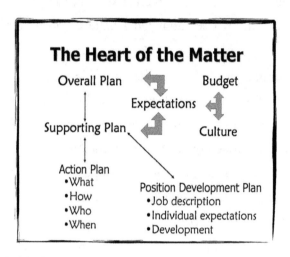

The Heart of the Matter

"The lower half of the diagram illustrates how the action plans and the PDPs support the business plan. I want us to discuss the importance of these two elements in taking the business plan and budget down throughout the organization, especially to our hourly employees."

George gave Gregg a concerned look, and Gregg nodded for him to speak. "I agree with you on principle. But how do you explain what is still so new to us to an hourly associate?" he asked. "I know I don't understand the full implications of concepts like the current ratio or the relationship of debt to equity. Right now they're still pretty meaningless words."

Gregg asked, "Didn't you take some of the development concepts we're adapting and apply them successfully to Willie and Ernest?"

George nodded.

"You can do the same using the financial concepts. If you think of less complex ways to explain these ideas, not only will they be clear to all the employees, they'll be clear to you as well. Part of understanding them is being able to explain them," Gregg responded patiently.

"I'll help by giving you an example I've developed," interjected Sally. "We've tossed around the idea of reducing our long term debt.

Gregg knows Don Paulus, our banker, has been pushing us to begin an accelerated repayment schedule, and with interest rates creeping up it is now essential that we generate more cash flow." Sally passed out her action plan to reduce debt and discussed the details with the team. "Now let's look at the PDP side of 'The Heart of the Matter.'"

"I'm accountable for generating a minimum of fifteen thousand dollars excess cash each month to pay down the principal. One of my actions is to work with George to reduce the amount of damaged goods in the warehouse because we have to eat the costs—and they are substantial."

George added, "Then we have to reorder the inventory and relocate the damaged goods, some of which have been sitting around for several years taking up valuable space. It's not only the damage to the inventory; there's also damage to forklifts and shelving. I've been trying to reach the point where I have the time to take care of it, but as we said earlier, another fire crops up and I became the fireman."

"George, that was yesterday. How can you stay in the present and deal with this issue? What do you need?" asked Gregg.

"More time and more hands, to put it bluntly," answered George.

Gregg could feel his coaching instincts rising and his adrenaline beginning to flow. "Well, we only have so many hours in a day and our labor dollars are at max. What specifically can be done to help you address this issue?"

George thought a moment, began to speak, and then stopped. It was as if a light bulb had turned on inside his head: his eyes brightened as he spoke. "I started to answer I would work harder; then I remembered us taking about working smarter. How's this? I will meet with Willie and Ernest and see what they think we can do to reduce the damages. I'll show them how much we have each month in damaged goods and the yearly total. That should get their attention."

"It's over thirty thousand dollars," Sally added. "That's two months of principal we could pay down with those dollars."

"How about if I use a different example with Willie and Ernest?" reasoned George. "They're both earning close to that amount in salary, and I know they'd like to earn more. I'll explain to them if we reduce the damages by ten percent, that's an extra three thousand dollars to improve the company's financial picture. And if the company is more profitable, there'll be extra dollars available for future raises. Knowing those guys, they'll say we can do better than ten percent."

When George completed expressing his strategy, the others gave him a round of applause and he stood up and took a ceremonial bow, grinning from ear to ear.

Gregg thought how wonderful it was that the pieces were fitting together. Intuitively he knew that soon there would be additional cash flow for the debt from reducing the cash outflow. And none of these accounting terms would have to be used to make it happen.

Next, he introduced the Rule of Three and was explaining how to handle the top three priorities and create a second tier of needed actions when George interrupted.

"Hold on a minute. If I create my top three priorities then I can have Willie and Ernest help me by showing them how to create their own top three? Man, we can raise some dust and get a lot of things accomplished! Why, we could take these priorities down to the hourly workers and get them involved. Sure makes sense to me." And with a final flourish, he added, "Glad I thought up all of this!" causing everyone to burst into laughter.

Maybe all this information isn't so overwhelming after all, Gregg mused. *If we all take it in bite-sized increments, we can manage the com-*

pany without feeling overwhelmed. And if we put the actions in priority, we'll more likely be accomplishing the right things in the right order.

"Okay, let's review what just took place," Gregg said to the group. "Sally started by explaining one of her financial goals. She brought George into helping her with an action—that is, reducing the amount of damaged goods. George reworded the accounting terminology into practical terms so that Willie and Ernest would understand the importance of their role in making this happen. When they buy into the idea, we ought to soon see progress and success in one area. Multiply these same principles throughout the organization and think of the benefits."

"Like college tuition for my son," Mike emphasized.

Nodding, Gregg continued, "As we've said before, it makes little difference if we're accomplishing these for personal or business reasons. The important outcome is for the company to be successful, and the only way that will happen is by following The Process. We're planning and communicating much better than we have in the past; and I expect, with good reason, that we will continue to improve. As we begin to truly understand our business, our costs and our human resources, and not only take responsibility for our actions but be accountable to each other for achieving them, we will earn a better return on our time investment." He ticked off his last three points on his fingers. "The development of our human resources will enhance the other actions we are taking. Tracking and measuring our success through our business plans and budgets will make us fiscally sound and ensure our future. Using the Rule of Three will keep us on track with our priorities."

The meeting came to a close on time with all agenda items discussed and follow up meetings set. "You know," Gregg said to George as the two left the conference room, "someone once told me that business should be fun. I'm beginning to see how that's true." He walked out of the conference room feeling a great surge of passion for his business and the lives it touched.

Epilogue

"And now it gives me great pleasure to recognize the new soccer champions for the league and their coach, Gregg Herbert," the announcer informed the teams and their cheering fans at the end of the season awards picnic.

Now that he had the time to coach, Gregg was thrilled to have been a part of the success of his daughter's team. He'd also gotten the opportunity to know her and her friends at a much more meaningful level. As he walked up to the podium to accept the trophy, he felt as if he were receiving it not only for a winning season of coaching soccer but one for coaching his company through its best year ever. The applauding audience was recognizing his interactions with the team, but in his mind he was also being congratulated for the interactions with his employees, and the resulting teamwork of both. He had come to realize there was not a great deal of difference between coaching soccer and coaching his business. Goals had to be set, strategies planned and executed, and everyone held accountable for their positions. But of all the attributes needed for a winning team, the players' passion to win was the most important, and that began with the coach.

The drive home was filled with chatter from the back of the SUV. Sitting in the passenger seat, Elaine squeezed his hand; the glow on her face told him all he needed to know.

"Did you see Mac at the picnic?" Gregg asked.

"No, I didn't know he was there," she answered.

"Oh, he was there all right, and I suspect he will be showing up on a regular basis. He gave me a thumbs up and a wink."

"I wish I could have thanked him for changing your life and making our family whole," Elaine said. "It is so good to have you back with us, instead of having an absentee husband and father. Gregg, I do believe you are looking younger—and you certainly are a lot more fun. I thought it would only last for a short time, but now I'm convinced your newly acquired knowledge and passion are a permanent part of your makeup."

At the advisory board meeting the next day, Gregg reported on the state of the company and brought the new advisors up to date on its progress. This was their first meeting; Gregg was following the agenda that had been mailed earlier in the month.

"As you can see from the financials you received, this is a record year for Herbert and Associates. Not only did we surpass our sales and profit goals, we have reduced our leverage significantly. Working with Don Paulus, we have been able to restructure our debt. Sally has agreed to stay on with the company and has accepted the role of vice president of finance.

"On the sales side, we have increased our territory by fifty percent and have added six new lines. We have been recognized as a 'Star Distributor' by our largest customer. I will also pass out an article that appeared in yesterday's trade magazine naming us the most improve company in our area.

"We will be purchasing the property next door to expand our warehouse. I am pleased to announce that George has been promoted to VP of logistics, and two of our foremen have been promoted to warehouse and assistant warehouse managers."

Following this summary, Gregg had invited eight recipients of the President's Award to meet the advisory board. "Ladies and gentlemen I would like you to meet these eight distinguished associates of Herbert and Associates."

Gregg introduced each one and gave a brief review of their position and how they had earned the award. When he introduced Willie and gave an evaluation of his performance, he added, "And this is the man that played a valuable role in my understanding of what really goes on in an organization and why our associates are our most valuable asset. For that, I will ever be grateful."

Gregg felt as if he were walking on air. He knew he would never do anything knowingly to regress to the past. He had Elaine to remind him at home and a passionate staff to keep him on the straight and narrow at work.

He was sitting at his desk the next morning eyeing the Mickey Mouse clock. It was a little before eight a.m. and the office was quiet. He had arrived early to catch up on some paperwork when he heard a knock at the door.

"Come in," Gregg instructed, wondering whom it could be.

"Gregg, so good to see you." Mac walked through the door, radiating his warmth inside the office. "I have a new 'visitor' I would like you to meet."

Gregg stood up, surprised, and walked over to Mac to give him a hug. He could see the satisfaction of a proud father on Mac's face.

"Good to see you are still wearing your gold star. You certainly have earned it," Mac praised.

"I wear it each day as a reminder of my promise to you and the company, as well as to me and my family."

Turning to Mac's guest, Gregg shook the confused-looking woman's hand and said, "I want you to know this 'trip' you have agreed to take with Mac will be the turning point of your life. But a word of caution: don't argue with The Man; his words are like the crown jewels. Listen to his knowledge with your heart and soul, and you will one day be in a position to fix the lives of those with whom you come into contact. It is a wonderful and rewarding feeling."

Then he turned back to Mac with a smile. "Okay, Mac. How can I be of service?"

- *DiSC* by Inscape Publishing
  www.inscapepublishing.com

- *Raving Fans: A Revolutionary Approach To Customer Service*
  by Ken Blanchard and Sheldon Bowles
  www.kenblanchard.com

- *Death by Meeting: A Leadership Fable...ABout Solving the
  Most Painful Problem in Business* by Patrick M. Lencioni

notes

notes

notes

notes

notes

notes

Printed in the USA
CPSIA information can be obtained
at www.ICGtesting.com
JSHW012022140824
68134JS00033B/2832